ATLANTIC OCEAN

CARIBBEAN SEA

INDIES

JAMAICA

PUERTO RICO (U.S.A.)

GUADELOUPE (Fr.)

MARTINIQUE (Fr.)

BARBADOS

TRINIDAD AND TOBAGO

Port of Spain

Barranquilla
Cartagena
Maracaibo
La Guaira
Valencia CARACAS

Panamá

Mérida
Ciudad Bolívar
Cerro Icutú 2800

Georgetown
Paramaribo
Cayenne

VENEZUELA

GUYANA
SURINAME FR. GUIANA

Medellín BOGOTÁ

COLOMBIA

Boa Vista do Rio Branco

GUIANA HIGHLANDS

Nevado del Tolima 17 110

ISLA DE MALPELO (Colombia)

ÉLAGO DE COLÓN
PAGOS ISLANDS) (Ec.)

Quito
Cotopaxi 19 347
ECUADOR
Chimborazo 20 561

Guayaquil

Iquitos

Leticia

Río Negro

Manaus (Manáos)

Río Amazonas

Río Solimões (Amazonas)

Equator

ROCEDOS SÃO PEDRO E SÃO PAULO (Brazil)

Belém (Pará)

São Luís (Maranhão)

ILHA DE MARAJÓ

Japurá
Putumayo
Juruá
Purús

Fortaleza (Ceará)

ARQUIPÉLAGO FERNANDO DE NORONHA (Brazil)

CABO DE SÃO ROQUE

Chiclayo

Trujillo

PERU

Nevs Huascarán 22 205

Río Branco

Pôrto Velho

Río Madeira

Tapajós

Xingú

Tocantins

Teresina

Natal
João Pessoa (Paraíba)

RECIFE (Pernambuco)

Maceió

B R A Z I L

SERRA DO PIAUÍ

LIMA

Callao

Cuzco

CHAPADA DE MATO GROSSO

Cuiabá

Brasília

Salvador (Bahia)

Volcán Misti 19 098

Arequipa

Mollendo

La Paz
Nev Illimani

BOLIVIA

Sucre
Potosí

Belo Horizonte

Diamantina

Pico da Bandeira 9482

BRAZILIAN HIGHLANDS

Vitória

Iquique

GRAN CHACO

PARAGUAY

SÃO PAULO

CABO FRIO

Antofagasta

Tropic of Capricorn

Salta

Tucumán

Asunción

Santos

RIO DE JANEIRO

ISLA DE SAN FÉLIX (Chile)
ISLA DE SAN AMBROSIO (Chile)

Copiapó

Corrientes

Iguassú Falls

Florianópolis

Coquimbo

Córdoba

Santa Fe

Salto

Pôrto Alegre

Valparaíso

SANTIAGO

Mendoza

Rosario

Río Grande

ISLAS DE JUAN FERNÁNDEZ (Chile)

A R G E N T I N A

La Plata

BUENOS AIRES

URUGUAY

MONTEVIDEO

Concepción

PAMPAS

Río de la Plata

Valdivia

Bahía Blanca

Puerto Montt

Viedma

Golfo San Matías

ISLA DE CHILOÉ

ARCHIPIÉLAGO DE LOS CHONOS

Comodoro Rivadavia

Golfo San Jorge

Monte San Valentín 13 314

WELLINGTON

HANOVER

FALKLAND IS. (ISLAS MALVINAS) (Br.)

Río Gallegos
Stanley

Punta Arenas

DESOLACIÓN

Estrecho de Magallanes

TIERRA DEL FUEGO

ISLA DE LOS ESTADOS

Mt. Sarmiento 8100

CABO DE HORNOS (CAPE HORN)

Drake Passage

SOUTH GEORGIA (Falkland Is.)

SOUTH SANDWICH ISLANDS (Falkland Is.)

SOUTH SHETLAND ISLANDS (B.A.T.)

SOUTH ORKNEY IS. (B.A.T.)

JOINVILLE

JAMES ROSS

ROSS

Antarctic Circle

ATLANTIC OCEAN

Longitude West of Greenwich

Relief		
Meters		Feet
3050		10 000
1525		5000
610		2000
305		1000
0	Sea Level	0
152.5		500
1525		5000
3050		10 000
6100		20 000

110° 100° 90° 80° 70° 60° 50° 40° 30° 20° 10°

10° 0° 10° 20° 40° 60°

Tres Esquinas
Puerto Leguízamo
La Chorrera
El Encanto
Arica
Iquitos
Benjamín Constant
Esperança
Leticia
São Paulo de Olivença
Santo António do Içá
Fonte Boa
Tefé
Coari
Codajás
Anori
Camará
Borba
Itacoatiara
Careiro
Manaus
Manacapuru
Barcelos
Carvoeiro
Moura
Tapurucuara
Taraqua
Pico da Neblina 3014
Mitú
Maués
Faro
Oriximiná
Óbi
Parintins
Itaituba

urimaguas
poto
Tingo María
Puerto Bermúdez
Pucallpa
Cruzeiro do Sul
Tarauacá
Feijó
Sena Madureira
Bôca do Acre
Lábrea
Humaitá
Sumaúma
RODOVIA
TRANSAMAZÔNICA
Eirunepé
S E L V A S
Porto Velho
Prainha

SERRA DO CACHI
SERRA DO DIVISOR
Abunã
Ariquemes
Rondônia
SERRA DO NORTE
SERRA DOS APIACÁS
SERRA DOS CAIABIS
SERRA DO TOMBADOR
SERRA

P E R U
CORDILLERA
Tarma
Jauja
Huancayo
Huancavelica
Ayacucho
Chincha Alta
Ica
Puquio
Nazca
Pullo
Abancay
Machupicchu
Cuzco
Quincemil
△ Nevado Ausangate 6384
Sicuani
Sandia
Ayaviri
Juliaca
Puno
ORIENTAL
A
CORDILLERA
Puerto Maldonado
Xapurí
Brasiléia
Cobija
Puerto Rico
Villa Bella
Guajará Mirim
Riberalta
Príncipe da Beira
Vilhena
Utiariti
Diamantino
Rosário Oeste
PLANALTO DO
MATO GROSSO
Cuiabá

Rio Branco
Río Branco

Camaná
Mollendo
Arequipa
Nevado Chachani 6075
Volcán Misti 5821
Puerto Acosta
Nevado Illampu 6362
Achacachi
Coroico
La Paz
△ Nevado Illimani 6402
Viacha
Corocoro
Todos Santos
San Joaquín
San Ramón
Magdalena
Santa Ana
Laguna Rogaguado
Laguna Rogagua
Reyes
Rurrenabaque
Apolo
San Borja
San Ignacio
Trinidad
San Javier
Concepción
San Ignacio
Mato Grosso
Porto Esperidião
Barão de Melgaço
Cáceres
Rondonóp

B O L I V I A
CHAPADA DOS PARECIS
CORDILLERA REAL
Oruro
Huanuni
Uncia
Colquechaca
Sucre
Zudáñez
Yapacaní
Quillacollo
Buena Vista
Cochabamba
Punata
Mizque
Portachuelo
Santa Cruz
San José de Chiquitos
Cerro Chochis △1290
Roboré
Puerto Suárez
Corumbá
Porto Esperança

CORDILLERA
OCCIDENTAL
TIPLIANO
DESIERTO DE ATACAMA
Tacna
Arica
Pisagua
Iquique
Nevado Sajama 6542
Lago Poopó
Salar de Coipasa
Potosí
Monteagudo
Lagunillas
San Lucas
Camiri
Vallegrande
Bañados de Izozog
GRAN CHACO
Pantanal de São Lourenço
Pantanal do Rio Negro
Aquidauana
Nioaque

C H I L E
S
Salar de Uyuni
Huanchaca
Pulacayo
Uyuni
Ollagüe
Volcán San Pedro 5974
Cerro Lípez 5929 △
Villazón
Rinconada
La Quiaca
Tupiza
Tarija
Villa Montes
Yacuiba
Mariscal Estigarribia
PAR AGUAY
General Eugenio A. Garay
Puerto Sastre
Carrería
Puerto Casado
Bela Vista
Porto Murtinho
Dourados

ARGENTINA
Abra Pampa
San Ramón de la Nueva Orán
Embarcación
Humahuaca
Cerro Saireácbur 5970

N

75°   70°   65°   60°   55°

Enchantment of the World

BOLIVIA

By Marion Morrison

Consultant: George I. Blanksten, Ph.D., Professor of Political Science, Northwestern University, Evanston, Illinois

Consultant for Reading: Robert L. Hillerich, Ph.D., Bowling Green State University, Bowling Green, Ohio

CHILDRENS PRESS ®

CHICAGO

A man near Potosî herding his cheerfully decorated llamas

Library of Congress Cataloging-in-Publication Data

Morrison, Marion.
    Bolivia / by Marion Morrison ; consultant, George I.
Blanksten ; consultant for reading, Robert L. Hillerich.
        p.   cm. — (Enchantment of the world)
    Includes index.
    Summary: Discusses the geography, history, people,
culture, politics, daily life, and economy of Bolivia.
    ISBN 0-516-02705-0
    1. Bolivia—Juvenile literature. [1. Bolivia.] I. Title.
II. Series.
F3308.5.M66   1988   88-10877
984—dc19   CIP
                                                        AC

FIFTH PRINTING, 1994.
Childrens Press®, Chicago
Copyright © 1988 by Regensteiner Publishing Enterprises, Inc.
All rights reserved. Published simultaneously in Canada.
Printed in the United States of America.
        5 6 7 8 9 10 R 97 96 95 94

Picture Acknowledgments
Root Resources: © Victor Englebert: 4, 47 (right), 107
(right); © Kenneth W. Fink: 25 (right); © Anthony
Mercieca: 27 (right); © Ruth Welty: 58 (left); © Victor
Banks Productions: 65 (right); © Irene E. Hubbell: 70 (left);
© Ulrike Welsch: cover, 92 (left)
Journalism Services: © Antonio Suarez: 5, 8, 59 (left &
right), 71 (top right), 72 (top right), 77 (right), 80 (left), 92
(right), 93 (right)
Marion and Tony Morrison—South American Pictures:
© Tony Morrison: 6, 10 (2 photos), 12 (left), 13, 15 (right),
17, 18 (right), 20, 22 (left), 23 (left), 24 (right), 25 (top &
bottom left), 26 (2 photos), 33, 35 (middle), 58 (right), 60
(right), 62, 63, 65 (left), 67, 74 (right), 76 (right), 79 (2
photos), 83 (2 photos), 86 (2 photos), 93 (left), 94, 95
(right), 99 (2 photos), 101 (left), 110; © Marion Morrison:
12 (right), 18 (left), 22 (left), 23 (center); © Kimball
Morrison: 41, 49 (2 photos)
© **Victor Englebert:** 14, 47 (left), 56 (top), 61, 74 (left), 75
(top), 76 (left), 81, 85 (right), 103
Nawrocki Stock Photo: © George Lill III: 15 (left), 23
(right), 75 (bottom left), 95 (left)
© **Chip & Rosa Maria Peterson:** 16, 56 (bottom right), 75
(bottom right), 77 (left), 91, 101 (right), 107 (left), 113
Valan Photos: © Paul L. Janosi: 24 (left); © K. Ghani: 27
(left); © Jean-Marie Jro: 59 (middle), 60 (left); © Anthony
Scullion: 100 (left); © Pam Hickman: 100 (right)
Shostal Associates: 31 (left), 80 (right), 108 (left); © Shaw
McCutcheon: 28 (top); © Hubertus Kanus: cover inset, 39,
53 (left), 68; © Eric G. Carle: 70 (right); © Kurt Scholz: 104
Odyssey Productions: © Robert Frerck: 28 (bottom), 31
(right), 84 (right)
Historical Pictures Service, Chicago: 35 (left & right), 38,
43
AP/Wide World Photos, Inc.: 52 (4 photos), 53 (right)
© **Cameramann, International, Ltd.:** 56 (bottom left), 71
(top left & bottom), 72 (bottom), 73 (2 photos), 78, 82, 84
(left), 85 (left), 89
Stuart Cohen: 72 (top left), 108 (right)
Len Meents: Maps on 54, 69, 75, 78
**Courtesy Flag Research Center, Winchester,
Massachusetts 01890:** Flag on back cover
Cover: Lake Titicaca, woman tanning hide
Cover inset: La Paz with Mt. Illimani in
                background

A blending of life-styles

TABLE OF CONTENTS

Aymara Indians at the foot of Mt. Illampu, patiently waiting for a lift from a truck to take them and their goods to market

Chapter 1

IN THE HEART OF
SOUTH AMERICA

The Republic of Bolivia is the only country in South America that has no water access to the sea. Bolivia is surrounded by Peru and Chile to the west, Brazil to the north and east, and to the south by Argentina and Paraguay. Covering 424,165 square miles (1,098,581 square kilometers), approximately the combined size of Texas and California, it is South America's fifth largest country.

The majestic, snowcapped Andes mountains run north-south through Bolivia in two ranges. Between the ranges, averaging over 12,000 feet (3,658 meters) above sea level, lies the mountain plain, or Altiplano, where over half of Bolivia's population lives and works. Lake Titicaca, the highest navigable lake in the world at 12,500 feet (3,810 meters) is at the northern end of the Altiplano. At the other extreme, in the south, the mountain plain becomes an arid wilderness of salt flats and volcanoes.

East of the mountains and covering more than three-fifths of the country is the *Oriente*, meaning "east," a low-lying land of forests, meandering rivers, and grassland. The region, though potentially rich, is populated only with small groups of forest Indians and a few hardy settlers.

Livestock grazing in the Altiplano

The Altiplano, or highlands, of Bolivia were once part of the Inca Empire. In the early sixteenth century, the Incas were conquered by the Spaniards who came in search of treasure. The Spaniards ruled for three hundred years until they were defeated in the wars of independence. General Simón Bolívar led the cause of independence and the last country to achieve independence—Bolivia—was named in his honor.

Chapter 2

LAND ABOVE
THE CLOUDS

Bolivia is in the tropics, but because of the altitude only the Oriente region has a typically hot, wet climate.

The mountains are very different. In the high altitudes it is hot during the day, and because of the clear atmosphere, the sun can burn severely. At night, temperatures often drop below freezing.

THE MOUNTAINS

The Andes are the backbone of South America. They run for about 4,500 miles (7,242 kilometers), from the Caribbean coast in the north to the icy Antarctic waters in the south. They are at their widest in Bolivia, where they divide into two ranges. To the east is the Cordillera Oriental, also known as the Royal Cordillera or Cordillera Real. To the west is the Cordillera Occidental.

The Cordillera Real is the older, higher range, with magnificent peaks that remain snowcapped all year. Standing like sentinels at either end of the range are Mount Illampu and Mount Illimani. Both are over 21,000 feet (6,401 meters). Illampu means Inca Storm God: it is an awesome mountain and reputably Bolivia's highest. Only the rare condor and tiny rodents live here.

Mount Illimani is Bolivia's most familiar mountain, because,

Snow-covered Condoriri (left) and Laguna Colorado, or Red Lake (right)

lying at its foot, in a deep canyon, is the capital city of La Paz, two and a quarter miles (3,621 meters) above sea level. Visitors to the city must take care to adapt slowly to the altitude, or they suffer from *soroche*, or mountain sickness.

Between Illampu and Illimani are many peaks, like the rugged Condoriri and the flat-topped Mururata. On Mount Chacaltaya is the world's highest ski slope and the world's highest cosmic ray station. The range, nowhere less than 18,000 feet (5,486 meters), creates a formidable barrier between the Altiplano and the Oriente, making transportation and communication difficult.

The western range, or Cordillera Occidental, is younger and of volcanic origin. It runs generally along the border with Chile. Dominating the chain is Mount Sajama, snowcapped and vying with Illampu to be Bolivia's highest mountain. Occasionally gases and vapors rise from the adjacent volcanoes, but none has erupted for many hundreds of years. The land around the volcanoes is dry, desertlike, and desolate.

THE ALTIPLANO

The Altiplano, which lies between the two cordilleras, is approximately 500 miles (805 kilometers) long and 80 miles (129 kilometers) wide. It has no water outlet to the ocean and is the largest region with interior drainage in South America. Except in the rainy season between January and March, there is little rain, and it almost never snows. Strong cold winds from the south regularly sweep across the plain, leaving dust storms in their wake.

Toward the end of the Ice Age, the Altiplano was covered by two huge lakes: Lake Ballivan in the north and Lake Minchin in the south. After the Ice Age, the lakes dried out. Today in the north, only Lake Titicaca and a few small freshwater lagoons remain. In the south, where conditions are much drier, nothing is left but Lake Poopó, some dried-out mudflats, and in the southwest, a series of salt flats. In the last twenty years a new lake, Uru Uru, has formed to the north of Lake Poopó. Lake Poopó itself is drying out.

South of the salt flats, at about 12,000 feet (3,658 meters), the land rises again to the Cordillera de Lipez, the southern barrier of the Altiplano. Beyond the Cordillera, forming part of the border with Chile, is the Puna de Atacama, a high-altitude desert of tough grasses, bogs, and volcanoes at 14,000 feet (4,267 meters). In this remote region lies Laguna Colorada, or Red Lake, its waters made a brilliant red by small algae that live under the surface.

Left: Looking east across Lake Titicaca   Right: The Titicaca frog

LAKE TITICACA

Lake Titicaca lies to the north of La Paz and forms part of
Bolivia's frontier with Peru. At 12,500 feet (3,810 meters), Titicaca
became the world's highest navigated lake when steamers were
first taken to the lake in 1872.

The lake is about 120 miles (193 kilometers) at its greatest
length by 50 miles (80 kilometers) at its greatest width. It covers
an area of 3,500 square miles (9,066 square kilometers). It
resembles an inland sea, and its shimmering blue waters are a
sharp contrast to the surrounding Altiplano and snowcapped
Cordilleras.

The lake is fed by summer rains and Andean streams. The
waters are cold and deep. The lake also has a legendary monster.
Expeditions have searched for lost cities and hidden treasure. In
recent years a Titicaca frog has been rediscovered. Almost ten-
inches (twenty-five-centimeters) long, it is one of the largest frogs

12

Totora reed boats on Lake Titicaca

in the world. An oasis for the wildlife of the area, many species of birds congregate on the lake. One species, the flightless Titicaca grebe, lives only on Lake Titicaca.

A favored habitat for all the wildlife is the totora reed that grows along the shore. There is concern that the habitat might be in danger. The Andean Indians have always used the totora for their reed boats and as thatch in their houses. Today the reed also is being used commercially in matting.

Many Indian families make their homes along the shores of the lake, where the land is more fertile. Rain falls more frequently close to Titicaca and the Indians can grow a greater variety of crops.

Islands dot the surface of the lake. The legendary origin of the Inca dynasty is associated with the largest island, the Island of the Sun. The lake itself is of supreme mythological importance to the Andean Indians, who believe their creator Viracocha rose from its cold waters.

The Yungas of the Cordillera Real below the mist-shrouded peaks

THE VALLEYS

The eastern slopes of the northern Cordillera Real drop very steeply from the snowy peaks to the eastern lowland plains of the Oriente. The slopes are called the Yungas. The vegetation on the slopes changes dramatically below the snow line. From about 11,000 to 3,000 feet (3,353 to 914 meters), the mountainside is covered with montane, or mountain rain forest. At the higher level, the trees are permanently cloaked in mist.

Everywhere on the mountain slopes there is the sound of running water. Waterfalls tumble over rocky ridges, and small streams become torrents as they make their way from the icy mountains to the lowlands to join a network of waterways that cross the eastern plains. Rain, which comes in from the Atlantic, is plentiful in this region, and the annual mean temperature is 60 to 70 degrees Fahrenheit (15.6 and 21 degrees Celsius).

Left: Aerial view of part of the city of Cochabamba, situated in a fertile valley
Above: Ichu grass on the puna

The slopes between 9,000 and 3,000 feet (2,743 to 914 meters) are well populated, as the land is fertile and productive. Many fruits and plants, native and introduced, grow in this zone. The coca plant, from which the drug cocaine is derived, grows abundantly here. Many trees useful for the timber industry also grow here.

At the southern end of the Cordillera Real, the slope is more gradual. The higher level is puna: flat, open, and barren. The land is only suitable for grazing animals. Lower down, between 2,000 and 5,000 feet (610 and 1,524 meters), is the area of "valleys," where rivers have eroded the puna rock. The valleys have been developed economically because they are good for agriculture.

In a valley, between 8,000 and 8,500 feet (2,438 and 2,591 meters), Cochabamba, Bolivia's third largest city, is situated. The climate is mild and the city avenues are lined with purple and pink jacaranda trees.

A street in Tarija

To the southeast of Cochabamba, in another valley, is the old city of Sucre. Founded in 1538, Sucre was the original capital of Bolivia and is still the legal and administrative center where Bolivia's Supreme Court meets.

A third city, Tarija, also lies in this zone, close to the Argentine frontier. It is claimed that Bolivia's best wines are produced here. Tarija is better known, however, as the place where bones of giant prehistoric mammals have been found—mammals such as mastodons, giant tapirs, and toxodons that are extinct today.

The Yungas and the valleys are Bolivia's most productive regions. But it is not possible to exploit the land to its full potential because of the formidable difficulty of transportation. The only way up and down the slope and in and out of the valleys is by road. In 1917 an attempt was made to build a railway over the mountains and into the northern Yungas, but it was abandoned after 94 miles (151 kilometers).

Chaco grasslands

The problem of communication also explains why the lowlands in the east of Bolivia have remained isolated and unexploited for so long.

THE ORIENTE

The Oriente is the vast area of Bolivia that extends from the foothills of the Andes east for many hundreds of miles to the frontiers of Brazil, Paraguay, and Argentina. From the foothills, the land slopes imperceptibly from about 1,476 to 656 feet (450 to 200 meters) or less. The only relief to the flatness is a few hills near the Brazil frontier. These lowland tropics cover about 60 percent of the country, but probably less than 15 percent of the population lives here.

This territory can be divided into approximately three zones. These are the tropical forest of the north, savanna country in the center, and Chaco grasslands in the south.

A rain forest in the eastern Andes (left) and a street in Trinidad (right)

The tropical forest is true Amazon rain forest, with tall trees, lianas (climbing vines), and dense undergrowth. Seen from the air, the deep rich green canopy is broken only by the brown water of meandering rivers.

The main city of this region is Trinidad, founded in 1686. Its historical origins are connected with early exploration by Spanish Jesuits, seeking to work among native Indians.

The savanna area is made up of tropical woodlands, including palms and coarse tropical grasses. Traditionally the great open Plains of Mojos to the north have been grazing lands for thousands of cattle. Recently, however, more attention has been given to commercial farming and the timber industry, particularly around Santa Cruz.

To the south, the savanna gives way to the Chaco grasslands. The Bolivian Chaco is the northern edge of the Grand Chaco, most of which lies in Argentina and Paraguay.

RIVERS

Only one river drains from Lake Titicaca. It is called the Desaguadero and it flows south some 200 miles (322 kilometers) into Lake Uru Uru, just north of Lake Poopó. There are no other major rivers on the Altiplano. Countless small streams, running from the snows of the mountains, feed the lakes.

The Altiplano has no outlet to the sea and the water evaporates in the very dry soil and air. In this way the salt lakes of the southern Altiplano have formed. The largest, the Salar of Uyuni, is 85 miles (137 kilometers) at its widest and about 100 miles (161 kilometers) long. A track across the Salar serves as part of the main highway between Bolivia and Chile.

On the edge of the Salar, workmen cut blocks of salt. They need to wear dark goggles to protect their eyes against the brilliance of the white surface. The salt blocks are stacked on trucks to be taken to the cities or they are carried by caravans of llamas to Indian communities in the mountains.

The Oriente is crossed by tributaries of two of South America's great rivers. In the north is the upper Amazon and in the south, the Plate River system. They start as tiny streams fed by mountain snows. When they emerge from the eastern slopes, they are already between 200 and 300 yards (183 and 274 meters) wide. The two largest tributaries are the Beni and Mamoré rivers, and as they cross the plains, they are fed by many smaller tributaries. The two rivers meet in the far north of Bolivia, where they become known as the Madeira River. The Madeira then flows 2,000 miles (3,219 kilometers) through Brazil to join the main Amazon River. The main tributary to the Plate River system is the Pilcomayo River, which has its source near the city of Potosí.

Channels of the Desaguadero River

Rivers are an important and, sometimes, only link between villages in the eastern plains. Early explorers traveled by river and some sections are deep enough to take paddle-wheel steamers.

In the nineteenth century, when the forest was being opened up for the rubber industry, all equipment came from Europe by way of the Amazon and its tributaries, a river journey that sometimes lasted fourteen months. Delays were often caused by dangerous rapids. On the Mamoré, in particular, a series of rapids extend over 200 miles (322 kilometers) into Brazil. In this location a hardy group of engineers began to build a railway to bypass the rapids. Many people died in the attempt, overcome by heat and disease, but eventually the project was completed.

SEASONS

The seasons most referred to in Bolivia are the dry season and the rainy season. The driest season tends to coincide with the winter months of June, July, and August. Similarly the rainy season occurs during the summer months of December, January, and February. But the rainy season has been known to extend into April. Sometimes there is also a mini rainy season in October and November. From June to August a cold wind called a *surassu* hits the Oriente. It comes from the frozen pampas of southern Argentina. The temperature drops by 20 to 30 degrees Fahrenheit (11 to 16 degrees Celsius) and storms lasting a week are not uncommon.

FLORA

Apart from small clusters of introduced eucalyptus, few trees grow on the Altiplano. The vegetation consists of tough grasses, bogs, and resinous plants.

The most common grass is ichu. Llamas and alpacas feed on ichu, and the Indians use it to thatch their houses. With so little natural vegetation, the local people have to use whatever they can. The spiky tola plant and a very hard resinous plant called yareta are used as fuel. The yareta is now in demand in the cities. Truckloads are ferried from the southern Altiplano and the plant, which grows slowly, is being used up quickly.

A most unusual plant on the Altiplano is the puya raimondii. In Bolivia it grows in just one location—in the foothills of the mountains—and is the tallest flower spike in the world. Its full height is 30 feet (9.14 meters). It is a bromeliad, and so is related to the pineapple. It flowers once in its 150-year lifetime, and then dies. When in flower, the puya has 8,000 blossoms and makes a good nesting place for birds. The stem of the dead plant is used as fuel.

Left: The puya raimondii, the world's tallest flower spike, grows on the slopes of the Andes. Right: Buttress roots of the oje tree

Within the misty world of the montane rain forest of the eastern slope, there is a huge variety of plants. Some that are familiar in the United States and Europe are begonias, passionflowers, geraniums, fuchsias, and orchids. Tree ferns and carpets of moss are everywhere. Some trees have medical properties. The best known is the cinchona, or quina tree, which gives us quinine, a medicine used against malaria.

Typical of the lowland rain forest are straight tall trees that reach to the canopy of the forest in search of light. Some have been known to grow to 150 feet (46 meters). Trees with large trunks have flanged, or buttress, roots to support them. Sometimes the trunks are smothered by climbing plants called stranglers. Ropelike lianas hang from the branches and the floor of the forest is covered with leaf litter.

The Chaco region in the southeast corner of Bolivia is a stark contrast to the rain forest. For most of the year it is a semidesert of

A huge, twisted liana (left) hanging from a tree, the yareta plant (center) which provides fuel, and a close-up of the cantuta (right)

thorny scrub, cacti, and scorched grasses. Then with the rains, which can be up to 40 inches (102 centimeters) in the summer months, parts of the Chaco turn into an impenetrable swamp.

The national flower of Bolivia is the cantuta—a red, trumpet-shaped blossom that grows in warm, dry valleys.

FAUNA

Andean animal life is not abundant and is not spectacular. It has adapted to survive in inhospitable territory, and can be difficult to find.

Llamas and alpacas have been domesticated for a long time, but their wild relatives, the vicuña and guanaco, survive in remoter areas of the mountains. The vicuña has been under threat for some years, as it is highly valued for its fine fur and skin. International efforts have been made to save the animal and

Capybaras (left), sometimes called water hogs, are the largest living rodents. Vicuñas (right) are now a protected species.

Bolivia has established the Ulla-Ulla National Reserve in the mountains near Lake Titicaca to protect the vicuña.

Deer and some small rodents also live in the mountains. Many of the rodents, including tuco-tucos and viscachas, seek shelter in burrows. Viscachas could be mistaken for rabbits, but are relatives of the chinchilla, the mountain rodent so valued for its fur that it is virtually extinct in the wild.

The fauna of Bolivia's tropical forests has been greatly disturbed in recent years. Some animals like the jaguar and ocelot have been hunted for their skins. So too have caiman—the South America crocodilian—and snakes. Large specimens of either now are hard to find.

The wildlife is affected when crews arrive to construct roads or drill for oil. The animals are hunted for food, particularly the monkeys, of which the many species include the black-spider and the capuchin, and their smaller relatives, the marmosets and tamarins.

Clockwise from above left: an agouti, a maned wolf, and a tapir

The heaviest animal of the Amazon forests is the tapir, which can weigh up to 300 pounds (136 kilograms). The world's largest rodent, the semiaquatic capybara, is also found here. Familiar forest species include opossums, armadillos, porcupines, and coatis. Less well-known animals are the tayra, paca, pacarana, and agouti.

A feature of some forest animals like the porcupine, monkey, sloth, and anteater is the prehensile tail. In time of flood, these animals can survive in the trees by using their tail as a fifth limb.

An unusual animal that lives in the Chaco is the maned wolf. It is not a wolf, but a rather specialized wild dog. It resembles a giant fox on stilts.

Many varieties of fish live in the lowland rivers. The best known, for its reputation as a "man-eater," is the piranha. But the piranha is less feared by natives and travelers than the smaller creatures of the river, such as the poisonous spine ray and the candiru, a tiny catfish with barbs.

The rhea americana (left) and the Andean condor (right)

BIRDS

Of all Bolivia's many bird species, the condor is the most spectacular. It is a large bird with a wingspan of up to 10 feet (3.04 meters) and is easily spotted against the snow of the Cordilleras. It is a much revered bird and is featured on Bolivia's national shield. Festivals are held in its honor and poems and songs have been written about it.

Another unusual bird is the rhea. It is similar to the ostrich and does not fly. Two species of rhea live in Bolivia. One, the rhea americana lives in lowland grasslands. The other, known as Darwin's rhea survives at 12,000 feet (3,658 meters) and higher. Just over 3 feet (.9 meters) high, the mountain species is the smaller of the two.

The rarest flamingo in the world lives on the Laguna Colorada in south Bolivia. It is the James flamingo and alongside it on the lake are Chilean and Andean flamingos. Around the Altiplano lakes there are Andean geese, ibis, gulls, and coots.

An Andean flamingo (left) preening its feathers and a cock of the rock (right)

The eastern forests of Bolivia are filled with the chatter of tropical birds. Toucans, parrots, and macaws are among the most colorful, and the brilliant orange of the male cock of the rock is stunning. Among the more extraordinary species are the curassow, guan, trumpeter, and the hoatzin, a primitive bird with claws on its wings. Along the riverbanks, herons, storks, screamers, and waders fish. The early morning chorus in the tropical forest is a lively event.

POTENTIAL

Bolivia has considerable economic potential. To date the country has lacked the funds and technology for development. Political instability and nationalization have deterred foreign investors. The government hopes to attract much-needed foreign capital back to Bolivia.

Above: Ancient Inca terraces used for agriculture on the Island of the Sun in Lake Titicaca
Below: Remains of observatories from the Aymara culture near Puna

Chapter 3

INDIANS, INCAS, SPANIARDS, AND BOLIVIANS

The Andean Indians who live on the Bolivian Altiplano today tell legends of their origins. The Aymara believe their god, Viracocha, rose from the cold waters of Lake Titicaca and created a world of darkness peopled by giants. When the giants angered him, he destroyed them. Then, reappearing from the lake, he created a new world, with sun, moon, and stars.

Archaeologists are not sure how or when man first appeared in the Americas. But it seems most likely that a migration took place from Asia across the Bering Strait toward the end of the Ice Age between twenty-five thousand and fifteen thousand years ago. Man made his way south and had arrived on the Altiplano about ten thousand years ago.

The earliest inhabitants of the high mountain plains were primitive hunters who also fished and gathered wild food plants. Few excavations have been carried out, but obsidian arrowheads shaped for hunting water birds have been found near Lake Poopó. Hunting was gradually replaced by simple farming. By 2000 B.C., several crops, including the potato, were grown. Llamas and alpacas were being domesticated, and the guinea pig was used as meat. Instead of moving around in search of game and fish, people began to settle in small villages.

The most populated area of the Altiplano was around Lake Titicaca. An archaeological site at Chiripa, on the southern side of the lake, has revealed a unique village with fourteen rectangular houses arranged in a circle. Materials used in the building were stone, mud bricks or adobe, and grass thatch. The people of the Chiripa culture used a variety of bone and stone tools, and made simple pottery.

TIWANAKU

The best known of Bolivia's ancient civilizations is Tiwanaku. According to some archaeologists, the influence of the Tiwanaku culture, with its artistically styled pottery and technological achievements, spread west from the highlands to the Pacific coast of present-day Peru. It was most powerful between A.D. 500 to 1000.

Most of all the Tiwanaku people were expert stonemasons and their work has survived on a site 12 miles (19 kilometers) to the south of Lake Titicaca. Archaeologists believe Tiwanaku, as the site is known, was a great ceremonial center, probably built between A.D. 200 and 500. It consists of a stepped pyramid called the Akapana that stands 50 feet (15 meters) high, a sunken temple called the Kalasassaya, and the Puma Punku, a stone-faced platform with walls 500 feet (152 meters) long. The stone used was sandstone and andesite and many blocks are impressively large. The largest stone block used in the Puma Punku weighs over 100 tons (over 9,000 kilograms).

Left: The Kalasassaya, a sunken temple   Right: The Gateway of the Sun

Legend says that when Viracocha destroyed the giants of his first world, he turned them to stone, and these are the carved megaliths resembling men that stand at Tiwanaku.

The best-known sculpture is the Gateway of the Sun, which is magnificently carved from a single block of stone. Along the top of the gateway an intricate carving with a central figure is sometimes described as Viracocha.

It is clear from the size of the Tiwanaku site, and the difficulty of transporting large stones from quarries several miles away, that the Tiwanaku civilization was well organized. The unsolved mystery of Tiwanaku is who built it. Many archaeologists believe it was fashioned by the ancestors of the Aymara Indians. But the Aymara, when asked by the Spaniards in the sixteenth century, denied any connection with the site, saying that "all that are there appeared overnight." The Tiwanaku civilization declined sometime after A.D. 1000.

PRE-INCA HISTORY

Before the time of the Inca Empire, the Altiplano was inhabited mainly by the Aymara, living in separate nations, each with its own ruler. These states were constantly at war with each other. The most powerful were the Colla and the Lupaca.

Two other tribes who lived on the Altiplano were the Uru and the Chipayas. The two tribes are referred to as the Uru-Chipaya because they shared the same language, Puquina.

The Uru were chiefly a fishing and hunting people, and the Chipayas were herders. A small group of Chipayas survive today in isolation among the salt flats to the west of Lake Poopó. The last Uru is thought to have died in the 1960s.

The Uru were known to be unfriendly and hostile. They claimed to be the oldest tribe in the world, according to legend "born before the sun." In earliest times they appear to have lived on islands in Lake Titicaca and in the swamps of the Desaguadero River. Later they were forced to move to the mainland where they lived in holes in the ground and in caves. Spanish chroniclers, encountering the tribe in the sixteenth century, described them as "so brutish they did not even consider themselves human."

Elsewhere other tribes, with different languages and cultures, existed, such as the Chicka and Lipez in the present-day department of Potosí, and the Yampara in the valleys near present-day Sucre. The region of Cochabamba was well populated by another linguistically separate group.

In the lowlands of the Oriente, forest Indians lived independently, fishing and hunting. They had little contact with the highlands.

These years before the Inca conquest are sometimes known as

Chullpas, or burial towers

the "chullpa period." Chullpas are burial towers built above the ground and many can still be seen on the Altiplano today.

THE INCAS

The Incas originated in Peru. They were one of several small tribes living near the present-day city of Cuzco in the Andes north of Lake Titicaca. Between 1200 and the middle of the fifteenth century, they developed and rose to dominate the other tribes of the region.

In 1438 the Emperor Pachacuti Inca came to power. Together with his son Topa Inca, who died in 1493, they expanded the frontiers of the Inca Empire to take in almost all of the Altiplano in present-day Bolivia. But the Inca did not conquer the tribes of the Altiplano without meeting fierce resistance.

About two years before Pachacuti, the previous emperor, Viracocha, decided to push south into Aymara territory. The rival chiefs of the Colla and Lupaca, on learning of the defeat of some

Aymara tribes by the Inca, sent envoys to Viracocha to seek his friendship. Viracocha favored Cari, chief of the Lupaca. This angered Zapana, chief of the Colla, who attacked Cari. Cari retaliated by killing Zapana. Emperor Viracocha then confirmed his alliance with Cari and the Lupaca.

But the rivalry between the two groups did not stop. Early in his reign, Pachacuti set out with his army and in a bloody battle successfully subdued the warring tribes. However, late in the reign of Pachacuti, a number of the Aymara tribes, again led by the Colla and Lupaca, rebelled. The uprising was a serious threat to the existence of the Inca Empire. It was the turn of Topa Inca to march south with his troops. This time the Inca succeeded in conquering the whole Colla province.

The Inca Empire was known as Tahuantinsuyu. It was divided into four quarters, centered on the capital city Cuzco. The southern quarter, which included the Altiplano in present-day Bolivia, was known as Collasuyu.

When the Incas acquired a new territory, they partly colonized it with their own people, while some of the conquered population were sent to other parts of the empire. Roads were constructed across the new province so that Inca officials could make regular visits.

The Quechua language, which the Incas used for administrative purposes, was usually imposed on everyone. The Aymara, however, were allowed to use their own language, and it survived not only the Incas but also the Spanish conquest.

The eastern plains of Bolivia were never conquered by the Incas. With peace established, life in the Collasuyu followed that of other parts of the empire. Inca administration was strict and effective. It was the responsibility of the appointed officials to

Emperor Atahuallpa *Francisco Pizarro* *Diego de Almagro*

ensure that the land was properly cultivated. The land was divided into three parts. Produce from the first section supplied the gods; the second provided for the emperor, the nobility, and the sick; and the third was for the peasants. In this way everyone in the Inca Empire was cared for.

THE SPANISH CONQUEST

Columbus discovered the Americas in 1492 and soon rumors of great wealth in the New World reached Europe. The Spaniards arrived in Peru in 1532 at a time when the Inca Empire was in a state of civil war.

Emperor Huayna Capac had died in 1525 and it was not clear who should succeed him, Atahuallpa or his half brother Huascar. When the Spanish captains Francisco Pizarro and Diego de Almagro first made contact with the Incas, Huascar had been killed and Atahuallpa was emperor. The Spaniards captured Atahuallpa and although the emperor's life was ransomed for a huge amount of gold, he was executed. With the death of the emperor, the people of the Inca Empire offered little resistance to the invading soldiers.

The first important Spanish visit to Aymara territory and south of Lake Titicaca was made by Almagro in 1535. One of his party, Juan de Saavedra, established the first colonial settlement at Paria, near the present-day city of Oruro. The Spaniards made themselves unpopular by using cruel methods to enlist Indians into the army and in time the Aymara, notably the Lupaca and Colla, rebelled. Francisco Pizarro sent his brother Hernando to put down the disturbances.

To administer his new colonies, the Spanish king appointed a viceroy as his personal representative. The present-day section of Bolivia known as the Altiplano, or Upper Peru, was part of the Viceroyalty of New Castile, later called Peru. The viceroy ruled with the help of a council or *audiencia*. The affairs of Upper Peru became the responsibility of the Audiencia of Charcas, centered in the city of La Plata, as Sucre was then known.

In the fifty years or so that followed, most of Bolivia's main cities, including La Paz, were founded. Upper Peru ceased to belong to the Viceroyalty of New Castile in 1776, when it became part of the Viceroyalty of the United Provinces of the Rio de la Plata, based in Buenos Aires, now in Argentina.

When the Spanish soldiers conquered the New World, they were accompanied by missionaries and priests who were sent to convert the Indians to Christianity. It is often said that it was these men of God and not the soldiers who conquered the Aymara. The first Dominican missionary arrived in Aymara territory at Chuquito on the shores of Lake Titicaca in 1539. Ten years later Dominican monasteries were in all the important Aymara towns.

The Dominicans were followed by the Jesuit missionaries who first settled in the Lake Titicaca region. Then they crossed the Andes to explore the eastern plains. The Jesuits are best remembered for their work among the lowland forest Indians. They built missions where the Indians were housed and fed. The Indians cultivated their own crops and learned to read and write, play music, and developed fine artistic and cultural skills. The Jesuits were expelled from South America in the 1760s, partly because other colonists envied their success, but examples of their superb Indian wood carvings still adorn many churches in Bolivia.

The Indians suffered badly under Spanish colonial rule. Many thousands died from epidemics and disease introduced by the foreigners. And those that survived were forced to work as slaves either under the *encomienda* system, which tied them to a particular colonist, or under the *mita*, a tax paid in the form of labor in the mines. Sometimes whole populations of Indians were moved to provide a work force in the mines.

Some priests protested about this to the Spanish monarch and in 1542 the "New Laws" were decreed to help protect the Indians. But it made little difference to the Indians' way of life, because in Upper Peru the Spaniards had found the riches they were seeking.

POTOSÍ

The great silver deposits of Potosí were discovered only a few years after the Spanish conquest, when in 1545 an Indian, said to be searching for a lost llama, chanced upon a vein of silver. Legend relates that the Inca Emperor Huayna Capac knew of Potosí, but forbade anyone to work the mine because a voice in Quechua had warned him, "Take no silver from this hill. It is

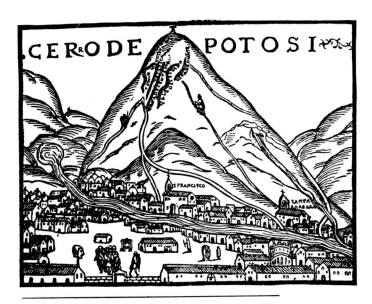

A drawing of Potosí from the sixteenth century

destined for other owners." The nearby mine of Porco was mined by the Incas, but they extracted the silver for use only in jewelry and ornaments.

The Cerro Rico, or Rich Hill, of Potosí, however, was exploited to provide the kings of Spain with the extraordinary wealth that funded wars and brought opulence to Europe throughout the sixteenth and seventeenth centuries. When the best ores were exhausted after the first thirty years, a refining process using mercury was developed. This made it possible to extract low-grade ores. As a result, the Cerro Rico was mined profitably for almost two hundred years. Situated at 14,500 feet (4,420 meters) in the Andes, the region of Potosí is cold and inhospitable. Yet virtually overnight a city was created.

Spaniards and foreigners arrived to make their fortunes, and African slaves were imported to work in the mines. Within one hundred years of the discovery of its riches, the city had a population of 160,000. It was the largest urban center in all Spanish America. Charles V of Spain bestowed on it the title of "Imperial City" with a coat of arms that read, "I am rich Potosí, the treasure of the world and the envy of kings." For the wealthy,

Potosí today, with Cerro Rico in the background

Potosí provided an extravagant life-style of parties and gambling. For the working poor, it meant misery and often death. Thousands of Indians died in the mines below the Rich Hill of Potosí.

END OF THE COLONIAL PERIOD

Toward the end of the colonial period, Upper Peru was rocked by insurrection and revolt.

After the conquest the population became divided into four different groups. The first conquistadores who had arrived in South America without families married the local Indians. From this intermarriage, the part-Spanish, part-Indian *mestizo* was born. Then there were those Spaniards born in Spain who had emigrated to the Spanish colonies. They were called *peninsulares*. Third, the pure-blooded Spaniards who were born in South America were the *criollos*. The last group was the pure Indians.

Early in the seventeenth century the peninsulares and criollos clashed violently in Potosí. In 1661 there was a mestizo uprising in La Paz, and again in Cochabamba in 1730.

The most significant rebellion occurred toward the end of the eighteenth century when the Aymara and Quechua Indians united in opposition to the colonial government. They were led by Tupac Amaru, said to be a descendant of the Incas, who urged the overthrow of the Spaniards and a return to the Inca Empire.

Although Potosí declined in importance in the eighteenth century, its prosperity had allowed the Audiencia of Charcas considerable independence in its relations with the Spanish crown. All Spanish inhabitants were called on to help quash the rebellion. But despite Tupac Amaru's capture and execution, the revolt continued for a further two years, during which the city of La Paz was besieged by some eighty thousand Indians for more than one hundred days.

Time was running out for the Spanish rulers. Not only was there growing resentment to local colonial government, but the Spanish colonies themselves had good commercial reasons for wanting to break with Spain. And there was support from the academic institutions such as the University of San Francisco Xavier in La Plata. Intellectuals from the university spread European ideas of liberty and they were directly involved in the first movement in the Audiencia of Charcas that led to eventual independence from Spain.

INDEPENDENCE

Events in Europe hastened the movement toward independence. In 1808 Napoleon Bonaparte of France invaded Spain and forced King Ferdinand VII from his throne. The breakdown of authority gave the colonies the chance to act.

From the first call for independence in 1809 until the creation of

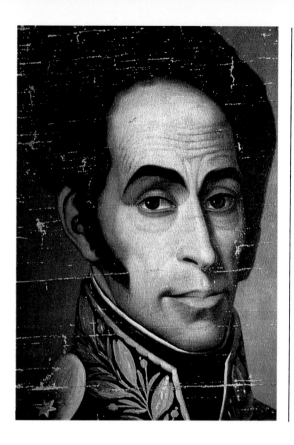

Simón Bolívar

the Republic of Bolivia in 1825, Upper Peru was in turmoil. In other parts of South America the independence movement was gaining momentum under Simón Bolívar in the northwest, and José de San Martín in the south. But in Upper Peru the royalist forces were led by General Pedro de Olañeto, a man of great loyalty to the Spanish king. And he was only finally defeated by Bolívar's general, Antonio José de Sucre, in the Battle of Tumula on April 2, 1825.

There was then some disagreement among the victorious generals as to whether Upper Peru should become an independent state. Simón Bolívar was doubtful. Sucre thought it should, while his second in command, General Andrés Santa Cruz, wanted to retain links with Peru. Sucre had his way and the Declaration of Independence was proclaimed on August 6, 1825. The new nation honored Bolívar by taking his name.

Chapter 4

THE MODERN REPUBLIC

In 1825 Bolivia claimed more territory than it has today. In the one hundred years that followed independence, the republic lost almost one quarter of its territory in the north to Brazil. In the south, an area of almost equal size went to Paraguay. Also, Bolivia's only outlet to the sea, through the Atacama desert to the Pacific coast, was taken by Chile.

EARLY DAYS OF THE REPUBLIC

Simón Bolívar led the fight for independence because he believed in freedom for all people. He was a man of enlightened ideas. One of his first acts as Bolivia's first president was to abolish slavery. At the time of independence, Bolivia's population was about 1,100,000. Nearly three-quarters of the people were Indian and many of them slaves.

But Bolívar did not stay long in Bolivia. He was anxious to return north to his native Venezuela. The first president of Bolivia was Antonio José de Sucre, who was succeeded by General Santa Cruz.

The misgivings Bolívar felt in creating an independent state of Bolivia were soon realized. For most of the colonial period, Peru and Bolivia were part of the Viceroyalty of Peru. Culturally and

General Andrés Santa Cruz

commercially the viceroyalty was the heart of the Spanish American Empire. As separate states, neither Peru nor Bolivia had the same power and wealth. Anxious to restore his country's authority, President Gamarra of Peru invaded Bolivia in 1828. Thirteen years of violence and chaos followed and further weakened both countries. Bolivia tried to take the port of Arica on the Pacific coast, which in colonial time was used by Upper Peru, but failed to do so. Eventually Gamarra was deposed in Lima in 1836.

Bolivia's President Santa Cruz, who favored union with Peru, then created a confederation between the two countries. Hostility to the confederation came both from within Peru and Bolivia. The confederation also was opposed by Chile, the republic to the south of Peru. It was not in Chile's interests to have one powerful nation on its north and west frontiers. In 1839 Chile sent its army into Peru and put an end to the confederation at the Battle of Yungay.

Once again on its own, Bolivia was ruled for forty years by a succession of strong military men known as *caudillos*. In effect they were cruel, ruthless, and greedy dictators who were constantly quarreling and vying for power. It was a tragic period in Bolivian history. It eventually led to the loss of the region that

From the 1860s, conditions in Europe had led to a renewed interest in silver—and in Bolivia.

Twenty years later there was a growing demand in Europe and the United States for tin, which was needed for the newly-started canning and automobile industries. Tin is often found in deposits alongside silver, and the Andes mountains of Bolivia proved a rich source.

Two political parties were created. The Conservatives governed from 1880 to 1899 and the Liberals from 1899 to 1920. By the time the Liberals arrived in power in 1899, tin had taken over from silver and made up more than 50 percent of the country's exports.

Other changes were also taking place. Whereas in previous years, politicians came from families with silver mining interests, the new tin barons were not openly involved with politics. They did, however, exert considerable behind-the-scenes pressure.

One of the most remarkable success stories anywhere in the world is the rise of Simón I. Patiño, the most famous Bolivian tin baron. From very modest beginnings in a small village south of Cochabamba, he became known throughout the world as "The Tin King." With only a limited education and little capital, he began his mining business 14,000 feet (4,267 meters) above sea level. After years of hardship and frustration, he discovered Catavi. The tin extracted from the Catavi mine made Patiño one of the richest men in the world. He controlled his fortune well, and bought other mines and smelters in many parts of the world. He also pioneered the founding of the International Tin Council, which controlled the world price of tin. Within Bolivia he funded hospitals and many charities. The Simon I. Patiño Foundation continues to provide students with scholarships in higher education.

The tin mines of Cerro Rico are underground with sweltering, cramped conditions.

The growth of the tin industry also had the effect of introducing a more cosmopolitan influence into Bolivian society. Foreigners came to invest and settle. In particular United States industry and financial institutions were attracted to Bolivia.

For some years the highland city of La Paz had challenged Sucre as the real center of power in the country. By 1890 some seventy-two thousand people lived in La Paz and that was the largest urban population in the country. It was three times larger than Sucre.

With the development of the tin industry, La Paz became even more important as the center of communication. The people of the city supported the Liberals. The citizens of Sucre backed the Conservatives. When the Liberals came to power in 1899, La Paz was officially made the capital city of the Republic of Bolivia.

The main job of the Liberals, particularly under their leader Ismael Montes, who was twice president (1904-8 and 1913-17), was to settle border disputes. A final treaty was signed with Chile in 1904. Bolivia relinquished all claims to the Pacific coast.

Five years earlier there was a different dispute. It involved the Amazon rain forest territory on Bolivia's northeast border.

RUBBER BOOM

Toward the end of the nineteenth century, rubber was in great demand in the United States and Europe for the growing automobile industry. When the hevea, or rubber tree, was discovered in the Amazon rain forests of Brazil, Peru, and Bolivia, a rubber boom followed.

The area was a long way from the Andean mining centers of Bolivia. In fact it was easier to contact Europe by river and sea than to make the overland journey to La Paz.

The only inhabitants of the Amazon region were scattered groups of Indians. They were drawn into the rubber boom as slaves and sent into the forest to collect latex from the trees. Huge fortunes were made, but the exploitation of the forest and native Indians was disastrous. Eventually the plight of the Amazon Indians was brought to the attention of the Western world by a young United States traveler. The end of the rubber boom finally came when rubber was successfully cultivated in Malaysia.

During the rubber boom, a dispute between Bolivia and Brazil led to the War of the Acre. The Acre was a region in the Bolivian Amazon, bordering on Brazil. The Bolivian government, so far from the action, could not do much. The Liberals, who were in power, decided to sell the territory to the Brazilians and use the money received in the settlement for the construction of the railroad network between Bolivia and the Pacific coast.

Left: An overseer with his Amazon Indian crew in the rubber forests around the end of the eighteenth century   Right: A nineteenth-century photograph of weighing and storing rubber before shipment

The need for the railway system coincided with the upsurge in interest in the mining industry. Bolivia had to find routes to deliver her minerals to the coast, for export to Europe and the United States. Chile agreed to give Bolivia access to the Pacific Ocean.

One railroad was constructed from the Chilean port of Antofagasta to La Paz, a distance of 700 miles (1,127 kilometers). The other, from Arica in Peru to La Paz, was completed in 1913. Both lines were funded by foreign capital, much of it British. The railways were major achievements of engineering, passing through some of South America's coldest, most windswept territory.

From 1920 to 1930 the Liberals lost control to the newly established Republican party. The peace of earlier years was disrupted by a battle for power between the leading Republican personalities. The rivalry took place against a background of a failing economy. The tin industry, in fact, reached record production levels in 1929. But it was at a time when prices were falling and the world depression of the 1930s was around the corner. It was at this moment that Patiño's International Tin Council saved Bolivia from complete disaster.

THE WAR OF THE CHACO

Bolivia entered the 1930s with both political and economic problems. And when another border dispute threatened, it suited the government to ignore its domestic difficulties.

The southeast corner of Bolivia is part of the large area of forest and scrub called the Chaco. The Chaco is said at times to be the hottest place in South America. The trees are tough and prickly. Apart from some native Indians and a few missionaries, no one lives in the northern section. Yet this region was the center of a most devastating war between Bolivia and Paraguay.

By the 1930s, Bolivia's only outlet to the sea was still by road or railway through Chile. At any time, Chile could cut Bolivia off if it wanted to. Bolivia needed another route to the sea, preferably to the eastern side of South America. Access to the Atlantic Ocean meant contact with Europe. A road through the Chaco could provide Bolivia with such a route. The road would connect with the Paraguayan river system, flowing into the Plate River and onwards into the Atlantic Ocean.

In the mid-1930s, rumors of petroleum deposits were circulating in the Chaco. President Daniel Salamanca of Bolivia decided to act. He deliberately provoked war with Paraguay. In the three-year war that followed, Bolivia lost 100,000 men. Many of them were badly equipped Indians forced from their highland homes to the frontline of the battle. In the peace treaty at the end of the war, Bolivia also lost more territory than Paraguay had claimed in the first place. An agreement was confirmed, however, that gave Bolivia navigation rights in Paraguay and Argentina.

MOVIMIENTO NACIONALISTA REVOLUCIONARIO

In 1936 Bolivia returned to a military rule for the first time since 1880. But as a result of the Chaco War, a new generation of politicians was born. Many people had been horrified by the treatment of the Indians during the war.

Although more than 50 percent of Bolivia's population were Andean Indians, they had no right to vote and they owned no land. In colonial days, they had been slaves in the mines and on the farms. Since independence, little had been done to improve their way of life.

The Movimiento Nacionalista Revolucionario (MNR) political party was created in the early 1940s. Its leader was Víctor Paz Estenssoro. The party came to power in 1952.

Bolivia was already well-known worldwide for its "changes of government." From the time of independence to 1952, it experienced 170 "palace" revolutions, or coups.

But 1952 was different. For the first time, a political party introduced a program of significant fundamental changes. The MNR planned to nationalize the tin mines. Everyone was to be given the right to vote. The large farms and estates were to be broken up, and the Indians would own land under a new Agrarian Reform bill.

The MNR policies were backed by the United States with financial and technical help supplied by foreign aid programs. It was only with the help of United States aid that the inflation that accompanied social reform was kept reasonably low.

Left to right: President Víctor Paz Estenssoro, President General René Barrientos, President General Hugo Banzer, and Bolivia's first woman president, Senora Lydia G. Tejada

The MNR lasted until 1964. In the end it failed because the economy could not support the radical reforms. The powerful trade unions challenged the government with strikes and disorder. President Paz was overthrown by Vice-President General René Barrientos, who was supported by the military.

INFLATION AND INSTABILITY

Since 1964 there have been many changes of government. General Barrientos was a popular president and the future might have been different if he had not died in a helicopter crash. It was during the presidency of General Barrientos that the Argentinean revolutionary, Ernesto "Ché" Guevara was killed while trying to organize peasant rebellion in the south of Bolivia.

Several military presidents followed, the longest serving being General Hugo Banzer from 1971 to 1978. Lydia Gueller Tejada was the first woman president who held office in 1979. Democracy returned to Bolivia in 1982 with the election of Hernán Siles Zuazo.

The Legislative Palace (left) in La Paz and President Hernán Siles Zuazo

During Siles's term of office inflation reached levels as high as 15,000 percent. The economy was further destabilized by the profitable cocaine trade. Repayments on foreign loans became more than income from legal exports. In August 1985, Victor Paz Estenssoro was again elected president.

Paz Estenssoro introduced anti-inflationary measures including elimination of government subsidies, a freeze of public sector wages, and privatization of government-owned business. Inflation and unemployment rates dropped sharply. In 1993 Gonzalo Sanchez de Lozada won the presidency. He promised to continue free-market policies which he initiated in 1985 as planning minister, as well as elevate the political status of the Indian population.

GOVERNMENT

Bolivia's constitution says that the president should be elected by direct vote every four years. If no candidate gains a majority of votes, the president should be chosen by Congress. Executive

power is vested in the president and a cabinet whom he appoints. Congress consists of a Chamber of Deputies with about 130 members and a Senate of 27 members.

Bolivia is divided into nine departments: Chuquisaca, Cochabamba, El Beni, La Paz, Oruro, Pando, Potosí, Santa Cruz, and Tarija. Three senators are elected from each of the departments. The prefect of each department is appointed by the president. Each department is divided into provinces, which are administered by sub-prefects. In turn the provinces are divided into cantons.

The constitution lays down certain democratic rules for the government of the country. But in practice these often have been ignored. For example, of the twenty-eight presidents of Bolivia between 1900 and 1971, only one-half have been elected by popular vote. Often the Chamber of Deputies and the Senate are closed down. The functions of the Chambers are then taken over by the Central Government.

Theoretically the judicial branch of government is independent. But appointments to the Supreme Court are often politically influenced.

Before the 1952 revolution, some 70 percent of the male population could not vote because they were illiterate. Women were prohibited from voting. There also were certain restrictions relating to property so that the number of people allowed to vote was very limited. After the MNR came to power, all adults over twenty-one years were allowed to vote.

NATIONAL DEFENSE

The republic has armed forces. Figures from 1993 show the army as largest with twenty-three thousand men, the air force with four thousand, and the navy with forty-five hundred.

As Bolivia is an inland country, the duties of the navy are restricted to Lake Titicaca and some Amazon rivers, where they patrol for smugglers and help river transport.

The MNR government in 1952 supplied the *campesinos* (native farmers) with guns, creating a peasant militia that lasted into the 1960s. All adult males of eighteen years may be drafted into military service. Certain military units have special tasks. The medical teams for national emergencies have jungle and mountain training. Ranger units are trained to combat terrorists and the Military Geographic Service is responsible for mapping the country. Much of the mapping work uses satellite pictures provided by Inter-American agencies.

Two branches of the police force have clearly defined tasks. The Transito is in charge of road traffic, driving licenses, and the roadworthiness checks of vehicles. The Transito also controls movement of traffic between towns by means of permits. The Department of Criminal Investigation is employed for major crime chasing and securing the state in times of political unrest.

Top: An Aymara Indian selling beans
and potatoes in La Paz   La Paz
University students in front of a bookstore
(left) and a woman at the market in Sucre (above)

Chapter 5

THE PEOPLE OF BOLIVIA

About eight million people live in Bolivia today, with three distinct groups. The largest of these groups is the Indians who make up approximately 60 percent of the population. This is a higher percentage than in any other country in South America. Indians include the tribes who live in the highlands, as well as the forest Indians of the lowlands.

The smallest group of people in the republic is the "whites." The whites are either descendants of the Spanish conquerors or European immigrants who have settled in Bolivia, particularly during the twentieth century. They represent about 14 percent of the population.

Mestizo is the name given to the third group who make up the remaining 32 percent of the people. Mestizos are the descendants of mixed marriages between the Spanish and the Indians. In Bolivia the name *cholo* is sometimes used, but cholo, or *cholito*, also refers to Indians who have left the country to live and work in the town.

AYMARA AND QUECHUAS OF THE ANDES

Aymara Indians have lived in the Andes of Bolivia since long before the Incas. Today most Aymara Indians live in the area of Lake Titicaca and around La Paz.

Two different styles of adobe houses with thatch roofs. Near the houses on the left are reeds stacked for use in making reed boats. An outdoor oven can be seen in the picture on the right.

Many of the Quechua Indian groups were moved into the region by the Incas as they expanded their empire south from the land of present-day Peru. The Quechua communities are mainly in the south of the country, around Cochabamba and Sucre.

Both the Aymara and Quechuas have their own language. In many ways the two groups of Indians are similar. They are simple farmers, cultivating a few crops and tending their llamas and alpacas. They are adapted to living at an altitude where the volume of oxygen available is approximately half the amount at sea level. These Indians are stockily built with barrellike chests. Their lungs are well developed and their blood is rich with oxygen-transporting red cells. All these features enable an Indian to run across high mountain passes with the ease of a healthy person at sea level.

Their houses are made of adobe mud brick with thatch roofs. There is one door and usually no windows. This is to keep evil spirits away as well as for warmth. The families eat, sleep, and live in one room inside. Often they cook there too, although some huts have outdoor clay ovens.

The Indians weave their clothes from the wool of the llamas and alpacas. They work on wooden looms and color the wool with vegetable and aniline dyes. Brightly colored skirts called *polleras* are the traditional dress for Aymara Indian women. The skirts are gathered at the waist and very full. Several skirts and petticoats are worn at the same time. At fiesta time, the polleras are made in fine materials and decorated with ribbons and sequins. Above the polleras the women wear rough cotton blouses, and, over their shoulders, a shawl called an *aguayo*. The aguayo is used for carrying a baby or goods to be sold in the market.

Aymara men have roughly made, baggy cotton trousers, which they cover with a long dull-brown colored *poncho*. Their knitted hats called *chullos* are designed for protection against the cold, with long flaps to cover the ears. Many men and women wear sandals made from the rubber of old tires.

Perhaps the most curious feature of today's Aymara dress is a bowler hat. Mostly it is the Aymara women who live and work in La Paz and are called *cholas* who wear these hats. It is believed the bowlers arrived in La Paz when British workmen came to

Different hat styles worn by the Quechua Indians

construct the railways at the beginning of the twentieth century.

Within the Quechua communities, hats are used to identify one village from another. Hats of all shapes and sizes can be seen at a local market. Some resemble the traditional Welsh milkmaid's hat. Particularly distinctive hats are worn by men from the small village of Tarabuco near Sucre. They are red and black and modeled on the helmets of the Spanish conquistadores.

Market days are important in Indian village life. People walk many miles from outlying villages to trade their animals and crops. The market is a meeting place, where friends get together and drink. But the market is also the place where goods from the nearby towns can be bought.

Even in the more remote parts of the Andes, Indian life is changing. The Indians now like to buy plastic buckets and bowls to replace their homemade clay pots and they put corrugated iron roofs on their huts instead of thatch. Many Indians own radios and bicycles.

Tin miners sometimes chew coca leaves to help them endure their terrible working conditions.

Indian life in the mountains is hard. Traditionally Andean Indians help themselves not to feel cold or hunger by chewing the leaf of the coca plant. They make a special paste of charcoal and lime to mix with the leaf, just as their ancestors did for hundreds of years. All Indians look forward to fiesta time, when they eat and drink well, and dance for many days and nights. At fiesta time they forget their many hardships.

THE KALLAWAYAS

The Kallawayas are a special group of Andean Indians. They are famed as traveling herbal doctors. Their home is in the mountains 150 miles (241 kilometers) to the northeast of La Paz, but they travel all over Bolivia dispensing medicines and curing illness. Many Indians believe that their illnesses are caused by evil spirits and they do not believe modern medicine can cure them. The Kallawayas use medicines and herbs from the mountain and

A Kallawaya herbal doctor and some of his helpers

lowland forests. They carry these in handwoven satchels. In the Aymara language *kallawaya* means "to carry medicine on the shoulder."

How the Kallawayas cure illnesses is a well-kept secret within their own community. They have been known to cure diseases like polio. But they do "read" coca leaves to find remedies and they rely on Indian superstition to help them.

THE CHIPAYAS

One small group of Chipaya Indians, descendants of the original Uru-Chipaya tribe, has survived in the extreme west of Bolivia near the Chile border. There are fewer than one thousand members of the tribe. The Chipayas were disliked by the other tribes of the Altiplano and were forced by them to live in the wilderness. The Chipayas claim they are the oldest people in the world and call themselves "people of the tombs." Their tombs are like small mud houses built above the ground. They call them

Chipaya women and children

chullpas. In the chullpas are skeletons that have the same style of hair and clothing that Chipayas wear today. Chipaya women plait their hair into hundreds of small braids. It is a custom that takes several hours and needs two or three women to help.

All Chipaya clothing is woven in natural colors of beige, brown, and black from the wool of their llamas and sheep. The women work on looms staked into the ground. Their clothing is a form of tunic without sleeves, worn over loosely spun trousers for the men. The women have crudely made blouses and shawls, and long black skirts.

As the Chipayas have few natural materials around them, their houses are primitive. They are built of mud and cut turf, with domed thatch roofs made from the tough Altiplano ichu grass. The one opening faces the side away from the prevailing wind. Because there are no trees or available timber, the Chipayas make the doors and roof supports from dried cactus.

Their village is quite unlike any other village in the Andes. The Chipayas exist by simple farming and herding of animals. But like the very early tribes of the Altiplano, they also hunt. In the salt marshes they catch ducks, geese, and flamingos. They hunt in a traditional way, with a *bolas*. A bolas is a Y-shaped cord weighted with stones at the three ends. Hiding in reeds and keeping as close to the ground as possible, the huntsmen wait for the birds to fly overhead. Then they spring up and, with amazing accuracy, throw the bolas into the air, where it catches the legs or body of the bird.

Unfortunately it was realized a few years ago that among the birds the Chipayas hunt is the James flamingo, the rarest flamingo in the world, whose habitat is the lakes of southern Bolivia.

In recent years missionaries and anthropologists have been working with the Chipayas. Of particular interest is the Chipaya language, Puquina. Puquina was widely spoken at the time of the Spanish conquest, but only the Chipayas use it today.

THE ORIENTE INDIANS

At one time the eastern provinces of Bolivia were the home of numerous lowland and forest Indians. The early explorers encountered many tribes when they first ventured through these lands.

The Oriente is still largely wilderness. And although present-day towns and settlements are widely separated, the lowland Indians of Bolivia have almost gone. The tribes have had contact with whites and missionaries for a long time. And four and a half centuries of exploitation from slavery to lumbering have drastically reduced the Indian population.

The few small groups remaining isolated are usually scared of intruders. Sometimes the Indians simply hide or they move deeper into the forest. Occasionally they respond by firing arrows.

Left: A Chipaya using bolas to hunt flamingos   Right: Fishing with a bow and arrow

Indians of the forest find their total daily needs around them. If they do not live completely naked, some tribes use bark cloth taken from local trees. The material is soaked to rot certain fibers, leaving behind only the strong parts. Bark cloth can be sewn with other natural fibers and even decorated using plant dyes. Bows, arrow tips, and spears are fashioned from hard palm wood. The arrow shafts are usually of bamboo. Some arrows, like those of the Siriono Indians, are over 8 feet (2.4 meters) long. There is an adequate supply of game, namely large rodents, wild pigs, and birds.

The people have known fire for a long time and they carry smoldering embers on their treks. By carefully blowing the embers against dry, soft wood, the fire can be rekindled. It is used for cooking meat, fish, and some jungle vegetables. Some Indians, like the Ayoreo of the scrub forests of the Chaco, consider armadillos a delicacy, and cook them whole in their shell.

Estimates vary for the number of people remaining totally isolated in Bolivia. Probably there are no more than a few hundred. But their existence will be threatened as roads cut deeper into the remote forests.

THE WHITES

Intermarriage between all groups in Bolivia has resulted in there being very few families of pure Spanish blood. The majority of "whites" are immigrants from Europe and Japan. In particular they are people of German or East European stock who arrived both before and after World War II.

Immigrants like the Japanese tend to be involved in agriculture and timber, while East Europeans run small businesses in the towns. The delicatessen trade in La Paz is almost all German.

THE MESTIZOS

Mestizos represent about one-third of Bolivia's population and the percentage is increasing all the time, as more Indians marry into mestizo families.

Depending on how much education he or she has received, a mestizo can be compared with the middle and working classes of other countries. The better educated mestizos are executives and professionals. They attend a university and sometimes travel overseas for further education. Many of Bolivia's presidents have been mestizos. On a different level, mestizos with only a limited education can get a variety of jobs. Miners, members of the armed forces, shopkeepers, teachers, domestic servants, and clerks all

A mestizo couple

come from mestizo families. A mestizo adopts western dress and customs: he or she usually rejects his or her Indian background.

Many mestizos are successful in commerce. In La Paz, the bowler-hatted cholas, who have market stalls or sell their goods on the pavements, are said to be some of the wealthiest people in the city.

LANGUAGE

Bolivia's first language is Spanish. It is the language of government and is used in the schools. Most Indians know some Spanish, but still use their native languages of Aymara or Quechuas, particularly in their songs and poems. Mestizos speak Spanish, but usually know one or more of the Indian languages. The Indians of the lowlands have their own languages. Some have rudimentary Spanish, which they have learned from missionaries. There is an Academy of the Aymara Language in La Paz whose aim is to preserve the purity of the Aymara language.

La Paz lies in a canyon at the foot of Mt. Illimani.

Chapter 6

EVERYDAY LIFE
IN BOLIVIA

Traditionally the majority of Bolivia's people have lived on the Altiplano. Urban populations center on the three main cities, La Paz, Oruro, and Potosí, that developed with the mining industry. Outside the cities, the people of the country work the land. The 1952 Revolution dictated that "the people of the country" would in the future be known as campesinos.

THE HIGHLAND TOWNS

The setting of the city of La Paz is magnificent. It lies in a deep canyon at the foot of Mt. Illimani. At the lowest level, around 10,500 feet (3,200 meters), are the finest residential areas with spacious houses with swimming pools, parks, and clubs and the highest golf course in the world. This lower end of the La Paz valley closes to a narrow passage locally known as "moon valley." Fine examples of "earth pillars," each capped with stones, have been left after centuries of rain erosion.

The city center lies between 11,000 and 12,000 feet (3,353 and 3,658 meters) and around the central plaza are the President's

Residential area (left) and an Indian market (right) in La Paz

Palace, Congress buildings, and central banks. High-rise buildings have appeared in place of small decorative colonial houses with iron balconies, which at one time lined the main streets. Most of the shops and offices are in this zone. Beyond, climbing toward the higher level of the canyon are the Indian markets. And lining the upper rim of the valley on every side are the gray shacks of La Paz's poor.

Making a living in La Paz is difficult. A high proportion of workers are government employees. The trade unions have their main offices in La Paz. Army and police headquarters are also there. But apart from these and other professions such as doctors, dentists, and lawyers, there is little opportunity for the ordinary man. Some become taxi drivers, but many of the unemployed have to work in odd jobs selling trinkets on street corners or cleaning shoes. Many people take on two or three different jobs.

Above: A shopping area (left) and an overview (right) of La Paz
Below: El Prado, the main avenue, has a lovely plaza as a central divider.

Scenes of La Paz clockwise from above: A bus in the downtown area, students demonstrating in 1986 against cuts in the education budget, and a narrow street crowded with traffic

Above: Bolivians strolling and relaxing on El Prado
Left: The University of San Andrés

Bolivia's principal university is in La Paz. The University of San Andrés has often been the center stage of revolutions. With the miners, the students have led many antigovernment protests.

To move around La Paz, people use buses or taxis. There is no subway system. Many of the streets are extremely steep. The police work the traffic signals by hand, so that the cars and buses coming uphill have priority. La Paz is connected to Bolivia's other major towns by rail, road, and air.

The towns of Oruro and Potosí have lost much of their previous importance. Potosí has architectural relics of its colonial greatness such as the Mint where most of the coins for the Spanish American colonies were made.

A cathedral (left) and a shopping district (right) in Cochabamba, the birthplace of tin baron Patiño

THE VALLEY TOWNS

Life is quiet in the valley towns of Cochabamba, Sucre, and Tarija.

Cochabamba is situated at about 8,000 feet (2,438 meters) above sea level and has an excellent climate. Surrounded by fruit orchards, it is the center of a thriving agricultural and dairy industry. The people of Cochabamba also work in small industries, such as the manufacture of shoes.

Sucre retains the atmosphere of a historic city. Local law says that all buildings must be painted in "colonial white." The city dates back to 1538 and there are many impressive colonial buildings. The university was founded by Jesuits in 1623 and is one of the three oldest in South America. The cathedral was built in the seventeenth century.

Above top: Sucre is called the White City, because by law most of its buildings must be whitewashed. Above: The courtyard of Sucre's University of Chuquisaca Left: St. Augustine Church in Sucre

On the Altiplano, many Aymara Indians use old methods for plowing (left) while others are fortunate enough to have new tractors (right).

THE COUNTRY—AGRICULTURE AND COCAINE

More than half of the people live outside the towns. They work either as subsistence farmers on the Altiplano, or in small holdings and plantations on the eastern Andean slopes. The staple crop of the Altiplano is the potato. After the harvest, the campesinos preserve the potato by turning it into *chuno* or *tunta*. They do this by a form of freeze-drying. First the women "tread" the potatoes to squeeze out the water, then the "dried" potato is left alternately in the sun of the day and the freezing cold at night. After this treatment, the potato can be kept indefinitely. By boiling in water, the product can be used like a fresh potato.

Native crops include *quinoa* and *canahua*, cereals that can be grown at very high altitudes, and *oca*, a tuber rather like a potato. Also grown are beans, barley, and alfalfa.

By 1984 and into the 1990s it was estimated that 75 percent of cultivated land was in cocaine production, most of it illegal.

Selling potatoes (left) in a Cochabamba market and coca leaves (right) in Santa Cruz

Government-controlled coca plantations are still part of the countryside scene in the Yungas valleys to the east of La Paz. The coca bush, with leaves containing about one part in a hundred of cocaine, has been cultivated since long before Inca times. The leaves are considered sacred and medicinal. The leaves are gathered, sun dried, and pressed for sale to the highland Aymara and Quechua Indians, who chew them. Long before the present drug problem, the government had a cocaine customs control.

International aid programs have been in Bolivia since 1952 helping with agricultural products and irrigation. They are currently concerned with the cocaine problem. There is a universal desire to stop the supply of cocaine, but it is recognized that this cannot be done without considerable hardship for the Bolivian people and the economy of the country.

Santa Cruz

COLONIZATION

Since the 1950s, much greater efforts than ever before have been made to open up the lowlands to the east of the Andes. Discoveries in oil and gas have led to a rapid growth in the population of the Oriente's largest town, Santa Cruz. In the 1950s it was a pioneering town of mud tracks and Spanish-tiled houses.

In the twenty years from 1950 to 1970, the population increased from 40,000 to 135,000. Today it is more than half a million. The people of Santa Cruz are known as the *Cambas*. Because of their tropical way of life, the Cambas are often said to be more like their neighboring Brazilians than the Bolivians of the Altiplano. Many people in Santa Cruz feel that their city should play a much more important part in the country's future. One of South America's best airports was opened there in 1984. Programs of colonization intended to move people from the highlands to the lowlands have met with limited success. The highland people have problems

Left: Adobe drying in the sun
Above: Settlements have been built in rain forest areas, as part of Bolivia's colonization programs.

adapting to the tropical climate. They are vulnerable to many diseases unknown to them in the mountains.

The difficulty of developing the lowlands has meant that amenities such as electricity and sanitation are often not available.

HOUSING

Materials used in building houses depend on what is available in each region. Traditionally the homes of Bolivian mountain people are made from mud adobe bricks. Clay mixed with water and straw is packed into molds and allowed to dry in the sun to make adobe. The blocks are sufficiently weatherproof to last many years. But to make the contruction more durable, the house can be faced with cement and sand. Many of the older buildings of La Paz were built in this way.

The shacks of the poor in La Paz are made from adobe bricks, usually painted only with a mixture of clay and lime. Today they have corrugated iron roofs, but generally are without electricity or

Modern high-rise buildings in La Paz (left) and native dwellings in the Amazon region (right)

sanitation. Because they are built on the muddy slope of the valley, they also collapse easily in heavy rainstorms. Every year several homes disappear in this way.

Elsewhere in Bolivia, where quarried stone is plentiful, the people build with stone and mortar or sometimes a stone base wall topped with adobes.

In modern construction of high rises, concrete, steel reinforcing, and bricks are customarily employed. In the lowland and warmer places, buildings may be as simple as a palm thatched Indian hut with a raised floor of split chonta palm or bamboo. Other materials used are wattle and daub, where a series of interlaced rods and twigs are supported with packed mud.

By contrast a sophisticated home in Santa Cruz may be a luxury dwelling of glass and brick complete with swimming pool and security television.

A rural school

EDUCATION

In colonial times, education was limited to men of the upper classes, who were taught privately or by the Catholic church. Some Indian people received instruction in arts and crafts from the Jesuits.

President Antonio José de Sucre decreed in 1828 that primary, secondary, and vocational schools should be founded in all departments. The law of January 8, 1827 was the first attempt at public education.

The MNR 1952 Revolution stressed the importance of educating all the people. Rural communities have been eager to cooperate with government programs to build centers of education or *nucleos escolares*. But in practice, children in rural areas are often prevented by distance or their family from attending school. The schools have little money even to buy pencils and books. Bolivia still has a high rate of illiteracy. The geographical distribution of

A mathematics class in a teachers' college

the people makes communication difficult, although teaching by radio is making headway. Teaching through radio schools is very important. Radio can reach every corner of the country where teachers, schools, and books are not available. An equal problem is language. Many of the Indian population not only have to learn to read and write, but they have to learn Spanish as well.

By law education is compulsory and free for pupils aged six to fourteen. There is a much greater opportunity for children living in towns to attend school. According to Bolivian government estimates for 1986, 1.4 million children attended primary level, and 225 thousand secondary level. There are eight state universities. Unfortunately many of the best students prefer to undertake their higher education outside the country.

Although most education is supported by the state, pupils can receive private education or attend Catholic schools. There are two private universities and one Catholic university.

Above: Indians worshiping Pachamama, Mother Earth
Left: The painting of the Virgin of Guadeloupe
in Sucre Cathedral is covered with 29,000 pearls,
21,000 diamonds, and emeralds and gold.

RELIGION

About 95 percent of Bolivia is Roman Catholic. Priests who accompanied the Spanish conquerors brought Christianity, built churches, and converted the people. Churches throughout Bolivia are open all day and regularly attended. Many of them are elaborately decorated with exquisite gold-leaf altars and colonial works of art. Perhaps the most valuable is a painting in Sucre Cathedral of the Virgin of Guadeloupe, covered in a priceless array of precious stones and gems.

Most Indians acknowledge the Roman Catholic faith, but have retained their pagan beliefs. Their gods are represented in the earthly world around them. In particular they honor Pachamama, Mother Earth, with libations and simple offerings, because they want her to bring them a good harvest.

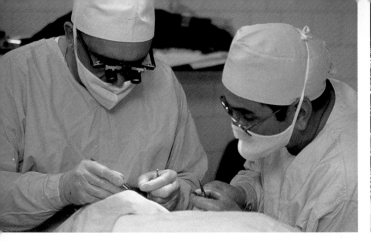

Left: Doctors performing cataract surgery   Right: Despite modern medicine, many people still believe in the effectiveness of herbal (or magic) remedies.

HEALTH AND NUTRITION

The most serious health problem is malnutrition. Children are undernourished and become ill easily. Foods high in protein, like meat and milk, are expensive and many families do without. Instead they eat mostly carbohydrates, like potatoes, rice, and bread. Fresh fruit is plentiful in the lowlands, but expensive and often in a bad condition by the time it reaches the highlands. Government and international aid programs try to teach the importance of diet and hygiene, especially to pregnant mothers.

Life expectancy in Bolivia is only sixty years. With the help of international agencies like the United Nations World Health Organization (WHO) and United National Children's Fund (UNICEF), malaria, yellow fever, and other tropical diseases have been reduced. Smallpox has been eradicated. There is no cure yet for a serious disease called chagas, which is transmitted by an insect's droppings.

Water, which is a carrier of diseases like hepatitis, is often contaminated and untreated. The Choqueyapu River in central La Paz is heavily polluted with domestic refuse, although in general garbage collection in the cities is adequate.

An urban family eating their main meal at noon (left) and two young sisters chatting with a cousin in one of the bedrooms in a rural home

The Ministry of Health is responsible for state medical services. In 1978 the government established a social security and health scheme covering 1,500,000 workers.

Most of the hospitals are in the towns. Rural medical clinics are scattered and badly equipped. In 1990 government figures recorded 5,100 doctors and about 15,000 hospital beds in various clinics. There are not enough dentists, and trained nursing staff often look for better jobs overseas.

THE FAMILY

A stable, close family unit is important in all levels of Bolivian society. The father is respected as head of the household.

Among the campesinos, young boys and girls are expected to work to help the family economy. A large number of children represents security. Grandparents live with and are cared for by the family. Less is expected of children from more affluent backgrounds. The bonds of wealthy, aristocratic families are useful in terms of influence and opportunity. Where there is no immediate large family, a relationship called *compadrazo* is sometimes created. This is similar to children having godparents.

85

During the seventeenth century, missionaries taught the Indians of Sucre to do beautiful, delicate carving. Since Sucre is a thriving community and proud of its antiquities, works such as the cedar wood carvings (above) and the pulpit (left) have been maintained in excellent condition.

Chapter 7

THE ARTS, FIESTAS,
AND RECREATION

Bolivia's culture has developed from the blending of Andean Indian and Spanish cultures. In colonial times the Catholic church produced most of the artists and writers. After independence Bolivia continued to be influenced by Europe. It is only in the twentieth century that a truly national culture began to emerge. In 1952 the MNR stressed the importance of involving the Indians in the national culture.

COLONIAL ART AND LITERATURE

Not a great deal is known about Bolivia's colonial paintings. The main schools were centered in Sucre, or Chuquisaca, as it was then known. The best-known painter, who worked in Chuquisaca in the second half of the seventeenth century, was Melchor Pérez de Holguín. The artists usually painted religious subjects. The Indians were taught by Spanish missionaries to sculpt and carve Christian objects. They worked in silver, wood, and stone. Examples of their talent can be seen today in pulpits, statues, and seats in churches and the cathedral of Sucre.

Most writers in the colonial period were monks and priests. Their writings describe the way of life before and after the

Spanish conquest. As the Incas had no form of writing, these chronicles are valuable records of this period of history. One of the best-known chroniclers was Nicolás Martínez Arsanz y Vela who wrote the *History of the Imperial City of Potosí*.

One of the very few scientific books produced was *The Art of Metals* by Padre Alonso Barba. It is a classic reference work on the metallurgy of the period.

Some missionaries who worked among the Indians wrote sympathetically of the native way of life and wrote dictionaries of the Aymara and Quechua languages.

When the new revolutionary ideas reached Upper Peru from Europe toward the end of the eighteenth century, the most influential writers were the three archbishops, San Alberto, Moxó, and Villarroel. Their work contributed significantly to the call for independence from Spain.

MODERN ART AND LITERATURE

The modern artists in Bolivia use native subjects in their paintings. The father of this school is Guzmán de Rojas. After studying in Madrid, Guzmán de Rojas returned to Bolivia and exhibited there for the first time in 1929. In 1930 he became the director of the National Academy. Guzmán de Rojas had many talents. He introduced murals to Bolivia, and through his restoration work, he "discovered" Pérez de Holguín, the painter.

In the 1940s Armando Pereira Pacheco produced *The Ferryman* (of Lake Titicaca) and *The Newsvendor* (an Indian woman). Rather more abstract, but still related to the Andean world, is the work of María Luisa Pacheco. One of her most powerful paintings is *Palliri*. It depicts a woman miner, kneeling in an attitude of

A powerful mosaic adorns the exterior of a cotton mill in Santa Cruz.

despair. Jorge Carrasco Núñez del Prado has exhibited abroad many times. He is perhaps best known for his *Painting at 4,000 Meters* (the approximate altitude of La Paz).

Other leading contemporary artists are Alfredo Da Silva and Alfredo La Placa. Among the successful, younger painters are Domingo Parada and Zilveti Calderón. Zilveti Calderón's works include many native topics, such as *The Virgin of Copacabana.*

The Bolivian sculptress, Maria Núñez del Prado has received wide acclaim internationally. She uses many materials native to Bolivia, such as *comanche granite,* guayacán wood, basalt, and onyx. Three of her most beautiful sculptures are *Black Venus, Spirit of the Cloud,* and *White Venus.* She once said that her aim was "to interpret the ancient soul of my country and our great Indian ancestors." Núñez del Prado has been called the Sculptress of the Andes.

There is a National Academy of Fine Arts in La Paz with courses in music, painting, sculpture, and ceramics.

The most interesting period of Bolivian literature coincided with the Liberal government of 1899 to 1920. In these years, cultural, literary, and scientific societies and magazines appeared. The outstanding writer was the historian Gabriel René Moreno, who spent much of his life in voluntary exile in Chile. He wrote the *Last Days of the Colony of Upper Peru.* Proud of his Spanish heritage, he criticizes Bolivia and is strongly prejudiced against the Indians. Despite this, Bolivia recognizes he was a great man of letters and has named the university in Santa Cruz after him.

Alcides Arguedas is one of the few Bolivian writers known outside his country. His works include *Raza de Bronce (Bronze Race),* and *Pueblo Enfermo (A Sick People).* He criticizes his countrymen, particularly the Indians, as weak and negative.

By contrast, two other writers and poets, Ricardo Jaime Freyre and Franz Tamayo cultivated the cause of the Indian.

Modern Bolivian writers are usually also politicians or diplomats. Probably the best known is Fernando Díez de Medina, who was minister of education in the MNR government. Others include Ricardo Anaya and Augusto Céspedes.

MUSIC

The mixture of Spanish and Indian cultures is expressed strongly in dances and songs. Dances like the *palla-palla* and the *morenada* make fun of the white man. The Indians dress in white masks to emphasize the point. The most popular dance inherited from Spain is the *cueca.* It is a graceful courtship dance of waving handkerchiefs and stamping feet.

The dances are accompanied by music played on a variety of instruments. Many Altiplano villages have their own percussion

An Altiplano village band

bands, which always include one enormous drum. Wind instruments like the *quena*, *tarka*, and *pinquillo* (forms of the flute) and the *sicu* (panpipes) are most common. Less well known, but still used in remoter villages, is the *pututu* horn, made from cow horn, and the *concha*, a sea shellfish.

Bolivians also play a tiny guitarlike instrument called the *charango*, distinguished by an armadillo shell on the back. Jaime Torres has made the instrument famous with his brilliant playing. He was a student of Bolivia's renowned classical charango player, Mauro Núñez. The Spanish influence remains in the guitars and violins.

Indian music has become increasingly popular outside South America and several groups play regularly to international audiences.

In La Paz there is a National Symphony Orchestra and, at the university in La Paz, a choral group specializes in Indian musical themes.

Left: Participants in a parade representing miners   Right: Ekeko, a good-luck figure

FIESTAS

The festivals and holidays of Bolivia have many different origins. Agricultural communities of highland and lowland Indian people celebrate their planting or harvesting seasons. Each town or village has a special festival for its patron saint on the saint's day in the religious calendar. Then such dates as the Day of Independence, battle dates, and Columbus Day are celebrated universally throughout the country.

Certain festivals stem from age-old Indian traditions. The Festival of the Cross on May 3 is a colorful mixture of dancing and ceremony for the Aymara Indians. All the villages around Lake Titicaca fill with people for the festival. The snowy Cordilleras around La Paz echo with the sound of flutes and drums. This festival has ancient roots in the Aymara tradition beginning long before the Incas.

The Devil Dance in Oruro's pre-Lenten carnival is about an evil spirit, "Supay," who is believed to exist in the center of the earth.

Alacitas is another Aymara festival in which everyone in the La Paz and Lake Titicaca region takes part. Alacitas has different dates for each area, but in the capital it is held on January 24. The most familiar object is a tiny figure, Ekeko, who brings good luck. Little figures of Ekeko, often made of silver, are sold in the Alacitas market. Ekeko is covered with tiny goods that may be household or personal. People, poor and educated alike, flock to the market to buy Ekekos and miniature items including cars and television sets. Out in the country the Indians build miniature houses and arrange tiny clay or metal animals in the yard.

The best known of Bolivia's festivals is the pre-Lenten carnival in Oruro, a mining town 160 miles (257 kilometers) south of La Paz. For a week of festivities, visitors throng the narrow streets. This festival is bound to ancient Aymara tradition and to the beliefs of the tin miners. Each year the miners seek protection by calling on good spirits and the Virgin of the Mines.

Music is provided by raucous brass bands. Hundreds of dancers

Examples of jewelry made by the goldsmiths of La Paz

in brilliantly colored costumes maintain a pace of gyrations and high leaping in the rarefied mountain air, which can exhaust people from sea level in a few moments. Some of the dancers wear enormous "devil masks" with horns and serpents. The eyes are fashioned from colored light bulbs.

In midyear at the height of the cold weather, the San Juan festival is celebrated in two ways. Fires are lit across the hillsides and in the doorways of houses. Then in a tradition carried from Europe, people leap over the fires to bring good luck—and a warmer month ahead. On the same date the older men of the Indian villages climb to high places where they perform ceremonies to placate the mountain spirits. For days after this festival the pungent smell of wood smoke and ash fills the valleys.

CRAFTS

With its wealth of tradition and recent history of immigration, Bolivia is renowned for craftwork. Indian weavers in the remote

Basketwork on display in a vegetable market, and an Aymara weaver (right)

valleys of north Potosí produce what is regarded as the finest weaving of its type in the Americas. Other skills of the original craftsmen include pottery, basketwork, and metalwork. Copper is beaten into urns and boiling pans. Silver is made into ornaments and jewelry. Goldwork, particularly examples of filigree, are a speciality of La Paz goldsmiths.

RECREATION

The national sport is soccer. Children play it on any spare patch of ground. The main ground is the Siles Stadium in La Paz, but the altitude puts visiting teams at a disadvantage, and matches are often played in Cochabamba instead. Bolivia meets other South American countries in the qualifying rounds of the World Cup.

There are facilities in Bolivia for playing tennis, skiing, sailing, and fishing. Malasilla Golf Club in La Paz is the highest in the world.

Few of the country's athletes reach international standards, although Bolivia was able to send a small team to the Olympics in 1984.

Chapter 8

A TROUBLED ECONOMY

Dr. Víctor Paz Estenssoro became president of Bolivia for the third time in August 1985. Inflation was approaching a staggering 15,000 percent.

Within eighteen months, the Paz government brought the inflation rate down to 60 percent. The Bolivian Congress set out a financial program to cut public expenditure and state-financed jobs. An agreement was reached with the International Monetary Fund for possible further loans. The exchange rate stabilized at just under 2 million Bolivian pesos to one United States dollar. Late in 1986 the government renamed the currency the *boliviano*.

With United States help, the government began to crack down on the cocaine trade. The illegal, but profitable, cocaine trade is valued at between 4 to 5 billion dollars. An estimated 600 million dollars is thought to come back to Bolivia yearly. In 1991 the country's legal exports brought in 819 million dollars. In contrast the foreign debt stood at more than 3.5 billion dollars.

MINERALS

Until recently tin was the mainstay of the Bolivian economy. After the MNR nationalized the mines, minerals continued to represent over 80 percent of all exports.

In the early 1980s, however, there was a sharp decline in the export of minerals, particularly tin. World prices and demand dropped. Production in Bolivia fell. Mining in Bolivia is physically difficult. Most of the mines are about 13,000 feet (3,962 meters) up in the mountains. Only people adapted to the altitude can work there efficiently. Since 1952 mining has been controlled by COMIBOL (Bolivian Mining Corporation). COMIBOL was disbanded by the Paz government and only allowed to work at district levels, provided it could show profit. The mines now provide about 4 percent employment. But transportation of loads and smelting processes are expensive.

The workers' interests were represented by COB (Bolivian Workers Central). It was a powerful force that every government had to reckon with. For thirty-five years COB was led by Juan Lechín, who helped bring the MNR to power in 1952. In September 1985, COB called a general strike in opposition to the government's austerity plans. Dr. Paz dealt forcefully with the strike and banished the leaders to the interior of the country. Juan Lechín announced his retirement in 1986. COB has collapsed and the workers no longer have a powerful organization to represent their interests. Even so, the government could be faced with considerable unrest if it does not find some solutions to the very high level of underemployment and unemployment.

In 1986 Boliva was a leading producer of antimony and tungsten. Gold is actively dredged from alluvial deposits in rivers east of La Paz. There also are deposits of copper, lead, and zinc. The country has large reserves of lithium and potassium, which have not yet been exploited. The government has plans to develop high-grade iron-ore deposits at Mutún, close to the Brazilian border. Bolivia is also putting more emphasis on local refining and smelting.

OIL AND GAS

The Standard Oil Company (New Jersey) first located oil fields in southeast Bolivia in 1927. Since then control of oil production alternated between the Bolivian government and private United States companies. Industries are now being privatized.

In 1969 Gulf Oil was extracting 40,000 barrels a day near Santa Cruz. The company was then nationalized and control passed to YPFB, the state oil company. YPFB accounted for about 60 percent of Bolivia's total crude production. Oil output had sharply fallen after 1973. In 1989 the Inter-American Development Bank (IDB) lent $56.9 million to develop the country's oil fields and increase production. Oil and gas supply 70 percent of energy.

Gas sales have become a main foreign exchange earner. About half the annual production of natural gas is exported by pipeline to Argentina. A pipeline to Brazil is under consideration.

HYDROELECTRICITY

Bolivia has great potential for the development of hydroelectric power. Between the snowcapped peaks of the Cordilleras and the Amazon plains, fast-flowing rivers cascade down the eastern slopes. Hydroelectricity has become a third source for necessary energy. There has been construction of dams on major rivers, which provides power to most cities. Another experimental project is to tap geothermal power from the natural heat in the earth in the volcanic western Cordillera. Test drilling has been carried out in the far southwest of the country.

Left: An oil refinery in Sucre
Right: Members of the Mennonite community of Santa Cruz

AGRICULTURE

About 60 percent of the population is involved in agriculture. Since the Agrarian Reform of the 1950s, campesinos have been able to own land. But they lack funds and technological knowledge. The Altiplano soil needs fertilizers to make it productive, and although tractors are occasionally seen, mostly the farmers use primitive wooden hoes, plows, and oxen. Some campesinos have formed cooperatives to jointly buy better equipment that they share.

Where agriculture has been advanced beyond the subsistence level, the land is productive. This is most obvious in the eastern lowlands where large areas of scrub forest have been cleared.

North of Santa Cruz, immigrant Mennonite farmers from the United States and Europe work the land. From the air a patchwork of large well-tended fields stretches for miles to the horizon. The dark earth is neatly furrowed and clean white painted settlements are connected by dirt roads.

Coffee berries (left) and a pawpaw tree (right)

A community of Okinawan immigrants also has settled near Santa Cruz. These people too, have added their agricultural expertise to opening up a wilderness and they are highly productive.

The best crops from this region are sugarcane, soybeans, and rice. These are traded in Santa Cruz and even exported in small amounts. In 1983 and 1984 a severe drought followed by floods resulted in a 60 percent decline in agricultural production.

Bolivia is rich in tropical fruits including bananas, pawpaws, grapefruit, oranges, tangerines, and avocados. At various times in the past, proposals have been made for exporting these fruits either as canned goods or as natural juices. Unfortunately all the economic forces have slowed this kind of development and canning is still largely for domestic consumption.

From a small corner in the northwest of the country, Brazil nuts are collected. These nuts come from some of the tallest trees in the Amazon forest. They have a high commercial value. After removing the shells, the nuts are dried in the sun and some are exported.

Left: Drying Brazil nuts in the Amazon region
Right: A family with its animals returning home at the end of the day

The Yungas and eastern Andean slopes have become intensively productive because of the demand for the coca leaf. Other crops include coffee, cacao, corn, barley, and yuca, or manioc.

LIVESTOCK

Throughout Bolivia animals are raised for food. With the exception of apartment dwellers in the major cities, most Bolivians keep livestock. Some city families have their own countryside plots where they keep chickens and pigs. The traditionally self-sufficient Aymara and Quechua Indians usually raise guinea pigs, a domesticated form of the wild Andean cavy.

Commercial chicken farming for meat and eggs has become part of the domestic economy, particularly around cities such as La Paz, Santa Cruz, and Cochabamba. The industry supplies the growing number of small supermarkets and delicatessen shops.

Development and aid programs of the 1960s with the cooperation of the Bolivian Development Corporation improved the dairy industry and now butter, milk, and cheese are distributed by road to the major towns. Local supplies of fresh milk are often insufficient to fulfill demand, so imported dry milk powders are reconstituted in Cochabamba.

Many small holdings keep cattle for milk or meat for family use or barter in the village market. Beef cattle are raised commercially mainly in the eastern lowlands. Some ranches extend from open savannas into dry tropical forest and the hardy cattle have to survive on poor, tough pasture.

Between 10 and 15 percent of Bolivia's land area is suitable for pasture. Usually the cattle are slaughtered on the ranches and the carcasses flown directly by cargo plane to La Paz and Cochabamba. Santa Cruz is supplied by beef driven for days on the hoof cowboy style. The by-product of hides and finely treated leather is used in local industries or by the shoe factories of Cochabamba.

Llamas and alpacas are usually kept for their wool. Just occasionally at Indian festival time, some llamas are killed and their meat distributed throughout the community. Sheep are kept in the mountains, but poor pasture and husbandry techniques have not led to flourishing farms. Like most of the other animals, they are used locally and an export market has never developed.

FISHING

Without a seacoast, fisheries in Bolivia are restricted to lakes and rivers. Fisheries experts have reported that the resources are good and with careful management could be of great value. The lowland rivers abound with many species including some medium-sized catfish of 22 to 44 pounds (10 to 20 kilograms), which are excellent food. In addition to the rainbow trout

Fishing with nets in Lake Titicaca

introduced into Lake Titicaca in the early 1940s, Lake Poopó was
stocked with Argentinean pejerrey in 1958. For a time they
flourished. But in recent years the size and the numbers of fish
caught have declined.

FORESTRY

Although more than 50 percent of Bolivia is forested, the timber
industry has yet to develop. The biggest drawback is the lack of a
seaport or easy way to export finished wood products to
neighboring countries.

Sawmills have been established outside Santa Cruz and
Cochabamba. They receive fine timber from the tropical forests of
the Amazon headwaters. Mostly the wood is used to satisfy local
demand for building materials, though certain hardwoods, such as
mahogany, are used for furniture.

A smelter in Oruro that produces antimony, a metallic element

Some of the finest quality chairs and tables are made from timber extracted from the Chaco forest or Chiquitos nearer the mountains. This huge area of dry woodland is the home of timbers like the guayacán favored by master joiners.

Another tree of commercial value is the quebracho. It is also known as "ax breaker" because its wood is so hard. Its bark is used for tanning and dyeing.

INDUSTRY

The small and largely Indian population restricts domestic demand, so few industries have been started.

Some of the most obvious products are specialized textiles for domestic sale. These products include the colorful striped cloth that Indian and Chola women use as a back sack for carrying their babies and market goods. Factories also produce blankets and sheets. Shoes are factory made in Bolivia and so are certain household items, though often from imported raw materials. Aluminum pots and pans are in this class.

Heavy industry and assembly plants have yet to arrive. A tin smelter and an antimony smelter on the Altiplano are a first step to developing the mining industry. Some small factories now produce an ever increasing range of plastic goods.

The basic materials for building, such as bricks and cement, are made in Bolivia. One cement factory is situated on the Altiplano at Viacha near La Paz. But with the introduction of high rises in the capital and some towns, there has been an increased demand for steel, which has to be imported.

Automobiles are imported from Brazil or Japan. Spare tires are imported and retreaded locally. The sugarcane grown in the lowlands is the basis for one of the major industries of Santa Cruz, where refineries produce sugar and alcohol. The alcohol industry has the potential of following in the footsteps of neighboring Brazil, where over one million automobiles run on alcohol.

Some processed foods are made in small factories, though the markets and shops are mostly stocked with imported goods. The last twenty-five years have seen little change in this pattern. Wine is produced in modest quantities in the southern Andean provinces and beer is brewed in several cities, often with a fine German tradition.

Pharmaceuticals are generally imported in bulk and packaged, with some items being locally produced. Perhaps in this field Bolivia may have a modest future as so many widely sought natural medicines can be found in the forest. Some pharmaceutical multinational companies have begun to investigate.

Chapter 9

BOLIVIA AND
THE WORLD

EXPORTS AND IMPORTS

Official figures show that Bolivia has a favorable balance of payments. Austerity measures introduced by Dr. Paz's government kept imports to a minimum. The Sanchez de Lozada government continues economic growth plans. Bolivia imports raw materials and consumer goods from Brazil, South Korea, the U.S.A., Argentina, European countries, and Japan.

Gas sold to Argentina accounts for almost half of Bolivia's total exports. Minerals are bought by the U.S., Germany, Great Britain, Belgium, and France.

Official figures do not reflect the huge revenue from the illegal export of cocaine. This revenue supports a black market of smuggled consumer goods that are not included in the official import statistics.

TRANSPORTATION

An efficient transportation network is vital to the development of Bolivia. The geography of the country has always made this difficult. Internally the Andes mountains create a formidable barrier between the highlands and lowlands.

Above: A road in the Cordillera Real
Left: The beginning of the descent
on the road that connects La Paz
to the Yungas valleys.

Externally Bolivia's only access to the sea is hazardous and relies on good relations with its neighbors. Agreements reached with Chile and Paraguay have been maintained. More recently Argentina and Brazil granted free-port facilities on the Atlantic Ocean, while a 1992 agreement with Peru provided access to the Pacific in exchange for Peruvian access to the Atlantic.

The Incas created good dirt roads into the southern parts of their empire, many of which still exist. The "wheel" was unknown. The emperor was carried in a litter, but peasants walked. Some of today's Indians still move between their villages and markets on foot, using mules and llamas to carry their goods.

One of Bolivia's most remarkable roads runs close to an Inca trail. It connects La Paz to the Yungas valleys. On one side a heavily forested precipice falls hundreds of feet into a deep gaping valley, on the other a perpendicular rock face soars into the sky.

Left: Many Bolivians in the Altiplano use whatever transportation is available.   Right: The train station in La Paz

Bolivia is dependent more on railroads than roads for access to the coast. From the time of their construction after the War of the Pacific, the railroads from La Paz to Arica and Antofagasta on the Chilean coast have continued to carry minerals and other exports. Imports to Bolivia follow the same route.

Other railway connections are from La Paz and Santa Cruz to Buenos Aires, with a change of trains on both routes. Santa Cruz also is connected to São Paulo in Brazil.

Buses are widely used throughout Bolivia, but they are often old and unrealiable. By necessity many country people cram into the backs of trucks to make the journey to town.

Bolivia has a national airline called Lloyd Aereo Boliviano, which has international flights to most countries in South America. Flights can be made to the United States and to Europe also, either directly or connecting with other airlines. Bolivia has international airports in La Paz and Santa Cruz.

Within Bolivia all important centers are connected by air. A small military airline, TAM, operates to remote parts of the country. Many small air-taxi services are available from La Paz and from Santa Cruz. Air transport is making an important contribution in opening up the eastern lowlands.

Until the arrival of air transport in the lowlands, the only means of travel was by river. Bolivia has more than 8,750 miles (14,082 kilometers) of navigable rivers that connect with the Amazon basin. Canoes and barges carry produce and passengers, but movement is slow and at times hazardous. Experiments have been carried out with Hovercrafts, but as yet this has not proved to be a practical means of transport in lowland rivers.

COMMUNICATION

At the present time there is freedom of the press in Bolivia. This has not always been so. In the early 1950s, the MNR closed down two newspapers—*La Razón* in La Paz, and *Los Tiempos* in Cochabamba—when they disagreed with government policies. *Los Tiempos* is on sale again. Censorship has been enforced at various times, particularly during military dictatorships.

Bolivia has more than a dozen daily newspapers. Six are published in La Paz, of which three—*Ultima Hora, Presencia*, and *El Diario*—are distributed throughout the country. *El Diario* is Bolivia's oldest newspaper. It was first published in 1904 at the time of the rise of the tin barons. Santa Cruz and Oruro each have two daily newspapers. Cochabamba, Trinidad, Potosí, and Tarija all publish at least one. The newspapers have a combined estimated circulation of more than 300,000.

A small number of magazines, mostly political, are published in Bolivia. Magazines from other South America countries and from the United States can be bought in La Paz and Santa Cruz.

Many more people listen to public radio stations, broadcast in Spanish, Aymara, and Quechua. Others are run by religious organizations. The Radio San Gabriel in La Paz broadcasts

Transistor radios for sale in a La Paz market

educational and religious programs entirely in Aymara. Radio can help to bring together the different regions and people of Bolivia.

Television has a similar role, but is restricted to the main cities and towns. There is one government and several private channels. Programs are mainly brought in from the U.S. and are in color. There is a university television service that produces educational programs. Many owners of sets now use video recorders. These are usually low-cost imports direct from the U.S.A. Television that is taped in Miami is passed around from home to home in Bolivia, complete with advertisements. Similarly, local television buffs have built dish aerials for receiving satellite programs from neighboring countries. Some poorer families form groups and buy a set between them for communal use.

An efficient telephone and telex system links Bolivia to the outside world. Direct dialing has recently been achieved. An automatic system works between most of the major towns in the republic.

The postal service works on a post office box number basis called a *casilla*. Each family has a casilla box in the post office and collects their own mail.

A small but enthusiastic group of filmmakers from Bolivia has received international acclaim. The group is called Ukamau and is led by Jorge Sanjines. Their films use as themes the exploitation of the Indians and the miners. Probably their best-known film was *Blood of the Condor*. Cinemas in the cities show international films soon after they are released in the United States and Europe. Bolivians enjoy films and the movie houses are always well attended.

A ROLE IN THE WORLD

Since 1952 Bolivia has received considerable financial and technical aid from international organizations and particularly from the United States.

Peace Corps and British volunteers worked with the United Nations and Bolivian government in *Acción Andina*, a program designed to help Indian communities with improvements in agriculture, medicine, and education. Other aid programs included a British agricultural team that was based in Santa Cruz. Members of the same team worked in the Yungas among the coffee growers. International missionary groups have made an important impact throughout the country, helping particularly with health care. At the same time the United States government channeled aid directly through the U.S. Agency for International Development (AID). Considerable technical assistance is presently being given by several European Union countries.

Despite this help, Bolivia has remained one of the poorest countries in South America. Bolivia's relations with the United States have been under strain because of the cocaine trade and Bolivia's foreign debt problem.

Diplomatic relations are maintained with many countries throughout the world. Over thirty countries have embassies in La Paz, and some have consular offices in Cochabamba and Santa Cruz. Bolivia is a member of various United Nations agencies, such as the WHO and International Labor Organization. It also belongs to the Organization of American States and the Andean Pact. The pact was formed with Venezuela, Colombia, Ecuador, and Peru to jointly plan the future development of the region. Bolivia participates in the trade agreements negotiated by the Latin American Integration Association.

BOLIVIA'S FUTURE

Bolivia is one of the poorest countries in the Western world and has many problems. Geographically the snowcapped peaks of the Andes are magnificent, but they present a formidable hurdle to progress. The great forests of the Amazon lowlands have enormous potential, but need large capital investment for development. Bolivia's concern with access to the sea is a constant hindrance to progress.

The country's dependence on only two commodities for export makes the economy even more vulnerable should one fail.

The peoples of the Andes have survived both the cruelty of colonial days and the hostility of the natural world in which they live. They are indeed a resilient people. The future of Bolivia now depends on the success of its government.

Political and economic stability is a first priority in attracting investment back into Bolivia. International investment alone can provide the capital to develop the natural resources. Bolivia's foreign debt repayments will have to be resolved.

Unemployment and underemployment are problems. If the mines are reorganized, many miners may lose their jobs. With improving education and movement to the towns, people are looking for better opportunities. The government has to try to provide these opportunities by developing industry.

As perhaps the least developed country in South America, Bolivia faces an uphill struggle. A course has been set by the government. If its aims can be achieved, then the future could be considerably brighter.

MAP KEY

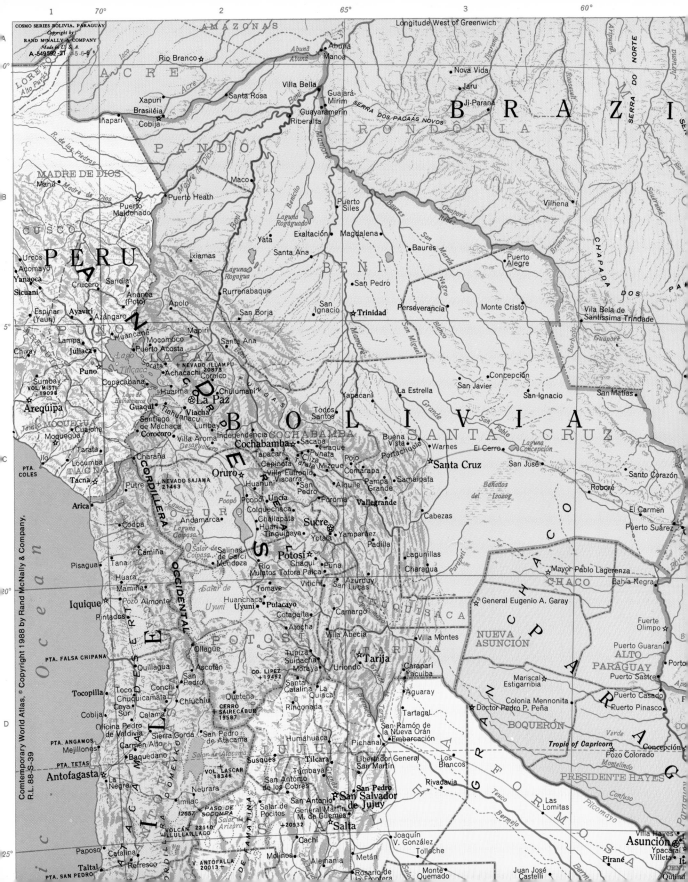

MINI-FACTS AT A GLANCE

GENERAL INFORMATION

Official Name: República de Bolivia (Republic of Bolivia)

Capital: Sucre (officially); La Paz (actual)

Official Language: Spanish. Most Indians, however, still use their native languages of Aymara or Quechua.

Government: Under the constitution of 1947, as restored in 1964, 1978, and 1982, the government has executive, legislative, and judicial branches. Executive power is invested in a president, a vice-president, and a cabinet.

The legislature has two chambers—a Senate and a Chamber of Deputies. There are 27 senators, three from each of the nine departments, elected for four-year terms, and 130 deputies, elected for four-year terms.

Bolivia's nine departments are administered by prefects appointed by the president to serve for four years. There are no local legislatures. Mayors, too, are appointed by the president.

The judiciary has a Supreme Court as well as district courts, tribunals, and other lower courts.

The constitution incorporated changes introduced after the revolution of 1952: the establishment of universal suffrage for all citizens over 21 (married women can vote regardless of age, however) and the abolition of the literacy requirement.

Religion: Ninety-five percent of the Bolivian people are Roman Catholic. The churches and cathedrals, many built during colonial times, constitute a national architectural treasure. Since the 1940s, the Catholic church has broadened its activities to include the fields of social aid and guidance. In the Indian communities of the Altiplano, some of the characteristics of pre-Columbian pantheistic religion have survived. Protestant denominations include the Methodist Episcopal church, the Baptists, and Jehovah's Witnesses. Judaism and Islam have a small number of adherents.

Flag: The state flag was adopted in 1888. It has horizontal stripes of red, yellow, and green. It has a coat of arms showing a breadfruit tree, a bundle of wheat, a mountain famous for its tin mines, and pictures a condor and an alpaca. The national flag has no coat of arms.

National Anthem: "Himno Nacional de Bolivia" ("National Hymn of Bolivia")

Money: The basic unit of currency is the boliviano. In March 1994, 4.53 bolivianos equaled $1.00 U.S.

Weights and Measures: The metric system is used, although in local markets both kilograms and pounds are used.

Population: Estimated 1994 population 8,171,000; 50 percent rural, 50 percent urban. Estimated 1998 population, 9,171,000

Cities:

La Paz	1,560,000
Santa Cruz	529,000
Cochabamba	403,000
Oruro	174,300
Sucre	106,300
Potosí	106,000

(Population figures based on 1990 official estimates)

GEOGRAPHY

Highest Point: Nevado Sajama, 21,463 ft. (6,542 m) above sea level

Lowest Point: 300 ft. (90 m) above sea level, near Fortaleza

Rivers: Most of the rivers of Bolivia are part of the Amazon River system. Wide, sluggish rivers flow through the Oriente, a vast lowland plain across the northern and eastern parts of the country. The Desaguadero flows south from Lake Titicaca, the only river that drains from the lake. The Plate River system is in the north. Its largest tributaries are the Beni and Mamore rivers, which meet in the far north and become the Madeira River. The main tributary is the Pilcomayo, which has its source near the city of Potosí. Rivers often are an important link between villages.

Mountains: The western third of the country is covered by the Andes. The mountainous highlands are made up of three distinct regions: the Cordillera Occidental, which rises along the Chilean border; the Cordillera Real, lying roughly parallel to it toward the east; and the Altiplano, a high plateau.

Climate: There is great diversity. Temperature and rainfall vary with the altitude. In general the country is colder and drier in the west and warmer and wetter in the east. The southern parts of the plains also are drier and cooler than the northern plains, where humid tropical conditions prevail.
In the Altiplano days are pleasant, with average temperatures from 50° to 60° F. (10° to 16° C). In the summer the temperature may rise to 80° F. (27° C) during the day. Nights are cold, with average temperatures of 30° to 40° F. (-1° to 4° C). Bitter winds may bring the temperatures even lower.
The Yungas, a small region northeast of the Andean Highlands, have a warm, humid climate. Most of the Oriente, a vast lowland plain, has a hot, humid climate.

The northeastern plains have a climate transitional between the hot and wet tropical areas of the Amazon Basin and the drier plains to the southeast.

The rainy season in most of Bolivia lasts from December through February.

Greatest Distances: North to south—900 mi. (1,448 km)

East to west—800 mi. (1,287 km)

Area: 424,165 sq. mi. (1,098,581 km²)

NATURE

Trees: On the Altiplano, where there is little rainfall, vegetation is scarce. In the higher valleys there are small trees and bushes, such as the molle (pepper tree), the chanar (a thorny shrub with sweet edible berries), and the pacae (a leguminous tree used as shade for coffee plants). The heights of the Yunga region are covered with great forests: green pine, black walnut, laurel, cedar, tarco (a shade tree producing masses of yellow-white flowers), sauco (which yields fruit used to make medicinal syrups), and quina (an evergreen tree yielding quinine).

Animals: Animal life resembles that of the neighboring areas of Argentina, Brazil, and Peru. The rain forest is an excellent habitat for snakes, crocodiles, and lizards, as well as for frogs and toads. Mammals include the sloth, monkey, jaguar, ocelot, opossum, tapir, armadillo, and anteater.

In the flat valley bottoms there are deer, armadillo, opossums, spectacled bear, and the tayra—a huge weasel.

Llamas and alpacas have been domesticated for a long time, but their wilder relatives, the vicuña and the guanaco, survive in remoter areas of the mountains.

Birds: Bird life is abundant in the highlands, particularly on Lakes Poopó and Titicaca, and includes geese, ducks, coots, cormorants, and gulls. The Andean condor is a New World vulture that is the largest flying bird in the Western Hemisphere. Another unusual bird is the rhea, which is similar to an ostrich and does not fly.

The rarest flamingo in the world—the James flamingo—lives in southern Bolivia. The eastern forests of Bolivia are filled with the chatter of tropical birds—toucans, parrots, and macaws are the most colorful.

Fish: Fisheries are restricted to lakes and rivers. Catfish and rainbow trout and the Argentinean pejerrey provide wholesome food.

EVERYDAY LIFE

Food: Potatoes, corn, and a grain called *quinoa* are staples of the Bolivian diet. *Chuno,* a dried form of potato, is used in stews and porridge. Corn-filled pies, called *humitas*, and meat turnovers called *saltenas* also are popular. Most Bolivians, however, do not have a nourishing diet. Some of them even depend on the leaves of the coca plant to relieve fatigue and hunger.

Housing: Most Bolivians live in very primitive housing made of adobe mud bricks with thatch roofs. There is one door and often no windows, not only to keep the dwelling warm but also to keep evil spirits away. The elite live in modern city apartments or in elegant, Spanish-style houses with patios.

Holidays:

January 1, New Year's Day
Monday and Tuesday preceding Ash Wednesday, Carnival
Good Friday
April 9, Bolivian National Day
May 1, Labor Day
Corpus Christi
July 16, La Paz Day
August 6, Bolivia Independence Day
November 2, All Souls Day
December 25, Christmas Day

Culture: The remarkable achievements of the Indian cultures of western Bolivia, notably those of the Inca and their successors, beginning in the first millennium A.D. (in architecture, metalwork, and textiles), are displayed in the National Museum and the National Museum of Archaeology, both in La Paz, and in the Tuahuanaco Regional Musem. Folk expression in music and dance has flourished for the last two centuries, and is seen especially in local festivals.

Pre-Columbian and Spanish-colonial instruments are widely used. Native music in its purest form appears in songs bearing the general name *aires indios* or Indian airs. The National Symphony Orchestra of Bolivia was established in 1940 under the auspices of the ministry of fine arts.

Development of literature and the fine arts was slow until the early decades of the twentieth century. The best-known painter, however, who worked in the second half of the seventeenth century, was Melchor Pérez de Holguín. A major subject of later artists was the social problems of the poor, depicted in the novels of Alcides Arguedas and Augusto Céspedes, the poems of Franz Tamayo, the paintings of Guzmán de Rojas, and the sculptures of María Núñez del Prado and Hugo Almaraz.

Some Bolivian filmmakers have received international acclaim. Jorge Sanjines is one of the most famous.

Recreation: Soccer is Bolivia's favorite sport. In the large cities professional teams attract large crowds. Tennis, skiing, and sailing are popular also.

Colorful festivals play a major role in the recreational life of the country. They feature parades, feasts, and elaborate dances.

Communication: At present there is freedom of the press in Bolivia, though the news media has been subject to military censorship during times of military rule. There are six daily Spanish-language papers in La Paz. Newspapers are privately owned. Among Bolivia's most powerful radio stations is the government-operated *Radio Illimani* —the Voice of Bolivia. Television programming falls within the province of the state-run broadcasting agency. Programs are largely brought in from the U.S., especially from Miami. The country also has several educational TV stations.

Transportation: Because it is landlocked, Bolivia depends on railroads, roads, and airlines. River transportation is not developed, partly because navigable rivers are in the least populated areas. Bolivia is connected with foreign seaports on the Atlantic and Pacific oceans by five railways. The most important paved highways are from La Paz to Oruro, Cochabamba to Santa Cruz, Santa Cruz to the north, and Cochabamba to Chimore. The Pan-American Highway crosses Bolivia, linking Argentina to the south with Peru in the northwest. Bus lines connect the principal cities. Lloyd Aereo Boliviano connects the principal Bolivian cities with international airports outside the country.

Education: The law of January 8, 1827, was the first attempt at public education. Civil education is divided into elementary, secondary, and university. Most education is state supported and is free, but private institutions are not forbidden. In some rural areas there are still no schools. Catholic, Protestant, and Jewish religious organizations are active in primary and secondary education.

One of the country's ten universities, the University of San Francisco Xavier in Sucre, is Roman Catholic. There are also institutions of higher learning at La Paz, Cochabamba, Oruro, Potosí, Santa Cruz, Tarija, and Trinidad.

The Bureau of Indian and Rural Education maintains rural schools for teaching trades and crafts. The national literacy rate is estimated to be about 63 percent.

Health and Welfare: There are three kinds of health services—those supported by the state through the Ministry of Health, those provided by the social security system for its facilities, and private clinics. In general the medical services and the hospitals in the cities are adequate. But in the rural areas both doctors and nurses are lacking. The most serious health problems are malnutrition, tuberculosis, prenatal and birth care, and tropical disease.

Principal Products:
Agriculture: Corn, potatoes, rice, sugar, wheat, coffee, cotton
Forest products: Timber, rubber
Manufacturing: Processed food, refined tin, textiles
Mining: Tin, natural gas, petroleum, zinc, lead, antimony, tungsten, copper, silver

IMPORTANT DATES

2000 B.C.—Hunters and farmers were living in the Bolivian area

A.D. 500-1000—Tiwanaku culture flourishes

7th to 11th centuries—Tiahuanaco Empire, first of the great Andean empires, extends over the Peruvian coast into the Altiplano region

1200s to mid-1400s—Rise of Inca civilization

1493—Inca Empire expands into present-day Bolivia

15th century—Bolivian region controlled by 12 nations of Aymara-speaking Indians

1530s—Spain conquers the area that includes present-day Bolivia

1545—Silver deposits discovered in Potosí

1661-1824—Indians in Bolivia periodically rebel against Spanish authority

1803-25—Decline in silver production

1809—Another unsuccessful revolt against Spanish rule

1825-29—Last Spanish forces are defeated by General Antonio José de Sucre. Bolivia declares its independence as a nation August 6, 1825 and elects Sucre as its first president

1828—Sucre is exiled; Peru invades Bolivia

1829-39—Andrés Santa Cruz is president

1836-39—Confederation of Peru and Bolivia engineered by President Santa Cruz; Chile declares war and breaks up the confederation

1879-83—War of the Pacific; Chile defeats Peru and Bolivia; Bolivia loses Pacific coast territory

1899—Discovery of tin by Simón Patiño

End of 19th century—Rubber boom

1903—Bolivia loses the Acre region to Brazil

Early 1900s—Railroads built to gain access to water

1920-35—Bolivia loses the Chaco War with Paraguay

1936-39—General unrest; President German Busch pushes through some reforms and then dies. The reform-minded Movimiento Nacionalista Revolucionario (MNR) party is born

1946—President Gualberto Villarroel is murdered, and various political leaders are exiled

1951—The MNR party wins presidential elections, but is prevented from taking power

1952—The MNR revolts and assumes control of the government, making Victor Paz Estenssoro president

1952-54—Bolivia undergoes one of the most sweeping revolutions in Latin America

1964—Military coup exiles Bolivian president Paz and puts in Vice-President General René-Barrientos as head of government

1969—Hugo Banzer Suárez comes to power and builds repressive regime

1978—MNR reemerges; Banzer resigns under threat of coup

1985—Paz returned to power; exacts extreme austerity measures; and the economy appears to improve

1988—Paz Government registers a trade surplus amounting to $22,000,000.

1989—Jaime Paz Zamora is inaugurated president; on the banks of Lake Titicaca at the site of the ancient Tiwanaku civilization, which flourished in Bolivia between B.C. 300 and A.D. 1200, archaeologists from the University of Chicago unearth a mass grave

1990—Paz Zamora signs an agreement with Bolivian Indian tribes to bar timber companies from felling trees in the rain forest where the tribes live

1991—Cholera cases are reported in villages near La Paz despite efforts to prevent spread of the disease by banning import of certain foods from Peru

1993—Gonzalo Sanchez de Lozada wins the presidency and continues austere economic reforms; an Aymara Indian, Victor Hugo Cárdenas, is his vice-president

1994—Former officials of the Paz Zamora government are called by Bolivian anti-drug authorities to testify on possible government involvement in drug trafficking

IMPORTANT PEOPLE

Diego de Almagro (1475-1538), Spanish soldier and explorer

Ricardo Anaya (1907-   ), writer and politician

Alcides Arguedas (1879-1946), novelist; his *Raza de bronce* tells of the treatment of Indians by Creole landlords

General Hugo Banzer Suárez, president of Bolivia from 1971 to 1978

Padre Alonso Barba (1569-1664), scientific writer; author of *The Art of Metals*, a classic work on metallurgy

Simón Bolívar (1783-1830), soldier, statesman, and revolutionary leader; known as The Liberator

Jorge Carrasco Núñez del Prado (1910-   ), contemporary painter

Augusto Céspedes (1904-   ), writer and politician

Fernando Díez de Medina (1908-   ), writer and diplomat

Lydia Gueller Tejada, first woman president of Bolivia, who served briefly in 1979

Ernesto "Ché" Guevara (1928-67), revolutionary leader killed in Bolivia while trying to organize peasant rebellion in south

Cecelio Guzmán de Rojas (1900-   ), twentieth-century muralist

Huayna Capac (d. 1535), greatest Inca ruler

Nicolás Martínez Arsanz y Vela, historian

Ismael Montes (1861-1933), lawyer, statesman, and soldier; president from 1904 to 1909 and 1913 to 1917

Gabriel René Moreno (1836-1908), historian and man of letters

Maria Núñez del Prado (1919-   ), contemporary sculptress; uses native materials for powerful, often tragic, figures inspired by Indian myth

Mauro Núñez, classical charango player

Domingo Parada, contemporary painter

Simón I. Patiño (1862-1947), industrialist and diplomat; operated tin mines; pioneered founding of International Tin Council

Víctor Paz Estenssoro (1907-   ), leader of MNR party, came to power in 1952; served as president from 1952 to 1956, 1960 to 1964, and was elected for a third time in 1985

Armando Pereira Pacheco, twentieth-century painter

Melchor Pérez de Holguín, seventeenth-century painter

Alfredo La Placa, comtemporary painter

Juan de Saavedra (1870-1939), jurist, president from 1921 to 1925

Daniel Salamanca (1869-1935), political leader, president from 1931 to 1934

José de San Martín (1778-1850), Argentinean soldier and statesman; helped Bolívar against the Spanish

General Andrés Santa Cruz (1792-1865), one of Bolívar's generals; president of Bolivia from 1829 to 1839

Hérnán Siles Zuazo (1913-   ), president from 1956 to 1960 and 1982 to 1985

Antonio José de Sucre (1795-1830), Venezuelan; one of Bolívar's generals; president of Bolivia from 1826 to 1828

Franz Tamayo (1880-1956), poet who began in the romantic tradition but became a modernist

Jaime Torres, player of charango guitar

Tupac Amaru (d. 1572), Inca chieftain

Zilveti Calderón, contemporary painter

INDEX

Page numbers that appear in boldface type indicate illustrations

About the Author

Newly graduated with a degree in history from the University of Wales, Marion Morrison first traveled to South America in 1962 with a British volunteer program to work among Aymara Indians living near Lake Titicaca. In Bolivia she met her husband, British filmmaker and writer, Tony Morrison. In the last twenty-five years the Morrisons, who make their home in England, have visited almost every country of South and Central America, making television documentary films, photographing, and researching—sometimes accompanied by their children; Kimball, seventeen, and Rebecca, eleven.

Marion Morrison has written about South American countries for Macmillan's Lets Visit series, and for Wayland Publishers' Peoples, How They Lived and Life and Times series. Resulting from their travels, the Morrisons have created their South American Picture Library that contains more than seventy-five thousand pictures of the continent.